S0-AZS-211

The Ambiguity of Change

The Ambiguity of Change

*An Inquiry into
the Nature of
Psychoanalytic Reality*

Edgar Levenson, M.D.

Basic Books, Inc., Publishers   *New York*

Library of Congress Cataloging in Publication Data

Levenson, Edgar A.
  The ambiguity of change.

Includes bibliographical references and index.
    1. Psychoanalysis.   2. Change (Psychology)   I. Title.
RC04.L475   1983   150.19′5   83–71018
ISBN 0–465–00121–1

Copyright © 1983 by Basic Books, Inc.
Printed in the United States of America
Designed by Vincent Torre
10 9 8 7 6 5 4 3 2 1

CONTENTS

Contents

PREFACE

PAUL VALÉRY, the French poet, said that the artist of modern sensibility must spend his time trying to see what is visible—and more important, trying *not* to see what is invisible.[1] Philosophers, he said (and he well might have added psychoanalysts), pay a high price for striving to achieve the opposite. The greatest obstruction to the practice of psychoanalysis is the tendency to read one's own theories into the patient, to create him in one's own image. That might not be too reprehensible a goal if we could count on the validity and constancy of our own precepts; or if, as psychoanalyst Donald Spence suggests, simply creating a mutually satisfying story with the patient were enough.[2]

But over thirty years of exposure to psychoanalysis have convinced me that we are, alas, as modish as the next. Many psychoanalytic dogmas seem in retrospect as dated and tied to their decade as the gray flannel suit or the miniskirt. If psychoanalysis has any timeless relevance, it cannot lie here. As I first said in *The Fallacy of Understanding*, accepting the analyst's particular view of the world, either as an aesthetic or as a profound reality, doesn't do the patient much good unless he leaves therapy far better equipped to deal with the complexities and ambiguities of life "out there" in the real world. The cardinal question for the patient may not be "What does it mean?" but "What's going on around here?"

It takes a considerable degree of alertness, sensitivity, and linguistic experience to grasp the nature of social interaction. This is by no means an automatic benediction of psychoanalysis as traditionally practiced, and its achievement may require a change in our concepts of the therapeutic process.

It has been my consistent sense that psychoanalysis is a powerful tool of influence and that it behooves therapists to distinguish carefully between the process and its outcomes. The latter, the goals of treatment, are inherent, tacitly or openly, in the metapsychology, which is no more than what the therapist believes. In *The Fallacy of Understanding,* I proposed that the power of psychoanalysis might lie in the "resonance" of expanding and overlapping patterns of experience. I would now carry this idea one step further. I consider that expansion of experience to be a prerequisite for the development of an instrumental skill, the ability to grasp what other people are doing, what has been done to you, what you have become as a consequence, and how that can be changed. I hope, in this book, to further advance that line of inquiry.

I must express my gratitude to those people without whose help this book would never have been written. I am very grateful to my editor at Basic Books, Jo Ann Miller, for her initial encouragement and her sustained and incisive editorial advice. The William Alanson White Psychoanalytic Institute, and particularly its director, Earl Witenberg, continue to supply the collegial atmosphere and intellectual stimulation that have made this book possible. Arthur Feiner, editor of *Contemporary Psychoanalysis,* the journal of the White Institute, and Darlene Ehrenberg, assistant editor, have contributed heavily to the development of many of these themes, as they first appeared in a series of journal articles. Certainly, all my colleagues and friends at both the White Institute and at the New York University postdoctoral program in psychoanalysis have contributed—sometimes unwittingly, albeit and perhaps even unwillingly—to this volume. My special thanks go to Nathan

Stockhamer, Edward Tauber, Steve Mitchell, and Magda Denes for their critical readings and support. Clare Powers, who prepared and reprepared the manuscripts, meeting impossible deadlines with unflagging good will, played an indispensable role. And, last, to my wife, Joanne, who stood by through all the usual teeth-gnashing and groaning, my gratitude.

The Ambiguity of Change

CHAPTER 1

Introduction

Laius was killed at a crossroads. . . .
Phocis is the country and the road splits
there, one of two roads from Delphi,
another comes from Daulia.
　　　　　　　　—SOPHOCLES
　　　　　　　　　Oedipus Rex

THE PATIENT, a thirty-year-old woman, experiences her first orgasm during intercourse. She suddenly becomes obsessed and angered over the sacrifices of time and money her husband has been making for his children of a previous marriage. Is she retreating from the experience of sexuality or intimacy, is she feeling freer to be self-assertive, or is she perhaps warily concerned that if she gives herself freely to her husband she will be exploited?

Another patient's first dream in therapy is that he is on a sailboat with his wife and children. The sailboat is in a narrow canal on his family's estate. The boat is capsizing, and he is terrified his small children will drown. Clearly he is worried about his marriage; clearly its being in difficulty is related to his involvement with his immensely powerful, controlling extended family. Will his marriage stabilize if he extricates himself from his family? Is his marriage an intrinsic part of his in-

3

volvement with his family—did he marry his wife because she fit the family image? Is he perhaps complaining that there has never been a real risk in his marriage or his life? Perhaps he's never put out to sea or taken an authentic chance.

Still another patient dreams that he and his therapist are in an arena, observed by a large group of anonymous people. The therapist is not aware that his own bare buttocks are visible. Shortly thereafter, the therapist reads to his professional colleagues a paper based on his treatment of this patient and is roundly attacked. Was the dream prophetic? Another patient, on the couch, notes that when he presents political views of which the therapist approves, he hears a grunt; when he states positions the therapist disagrees with, there is silence. The therapist has been caught out and confesses. How should the interaction proceed? Is it an unfortunate aberrance to be resolved and put aside; is it a characteristic response called out by the patient in others; is it a masochistic submission by the patient to have withheld his perception so long? Or is it an act of covert aggression?

These vignettes, some of which will be expanded later, are extracted from clinical material. On the basis of their response to this material, psychoanalysts line up into markedly factional groups. Yet, in spite of all the dissension, we are left with a sneaking feeling that somehow we are all doing much the same thing, albeit subsumed under different theoretical sets and, perhaps, with different goals in mind. Like a feuding family, we acknowledge begrudgingly a family resemblance. It is the nature of the common ground of psychoanalysis and its subsequent ramifications that is the topic of this book. For the moment, the material serves to illustrate the ambiguity that transcends and blurs the traditional categories of psychoanalytic data: that is, material about the patient's history and present life, transference, and countertransference. Is the patient disabled by an anachronistic infantile fantasy system or by an uncomprehended reality? Does cure require insight, participation, risk taking? What use should be made of the patient's perceptions of the therapist, the therapist's perceptions of the patient and of himself in interaction with the patient? Should countertransference be exculpated or can it be utilized as a therapeutic instrument? What is cure and when is it ideological persuasion?

It is evident that there are vast differences among psychoanalysts in their perception and uses of these issues, which, if not ultimately resolvable, are, at the very least, orienting. The problem resides in the nature of psychoanalysis, which may be viewed not as a unique phenomenon but as one of that large group of activities that are both performed and talked about. The gap between what is done and what can be known and said about what is done is the epistemological dilemma.

As in any complex activity, the relationship between theory and practice is obscure. This is patently obvious to anyone who has ever learned a skill, practiced a sport, or undertaken an artistic endeavor. In these activities, common sense dictates that the conceptual/activity gap be taken for granted, and it is understood that teaching provides only an armature for a much more complex and elusive learning activity, dependent on preceptorship, personal cognitive style, and talent. Somewhere in the interstices between the theory and the act lies the art of teaching.

It is only when science enters the field that this heretofore rather comfortable discrepancy becomes an embarrassment. Psychoanalysis lays claim to scientific credentials, and rightly so: it is an effort to establish a systematic theoretical structure that operates with consistency and predictability in the phenomenal world. Unlike medicine men and magicians, psychoanalysts are not content to set their stages, arrange their props, and then hope that something happens. We aim for a much more determinate relationship between theory and practice. More precisely, we believe that our theory should define and dictate the technique of therapy. To that end, psychoanalysts do not talk simply of "psychoanalytic" theory, but of "metapsychology," a grander and vastly more encompassing conceit, which attempts an orchestration of clinical concepts with all philosophical aspects of mental processes; "mind-body relationship, origin and purpose of the mind, and similar speculations that are beyond the reach of empirical verification."[1]

Clearly, this desideratum is yet to be achieved. Anna Freud said that "[theory] . . . has become the bugbear of the clinically oriented analyst who feels wholly divorced from it."[2] There has been no paucity of equally disenchanted recent comments. According to Masud Khan, "Psychoanalysis today is facing a crisis from within: a crisis of stasis. There is an irrefutable disparity between its theories and its clinical practices."[3] Analysts find themselves using metapsychology as a private language, a Guild identification that permits them to talk to their colleagues and to write in their journals. Analysts of all persuasions continue to treat their patients with a considerable degree of success (at least in the subjective assessment of both participants) and yet are hard put to know exactly how to talk about what it is they do when they do what they know how to do. This ineffable competence can be defined as the *praxis* of psychoanalysis: not the theory, or metapsychology, or even the theory of therapy, but the *act* of psychoanalysis.

Eschewing theory, the analyst can proceed with his work like the fabled centipede, tripping along hopefully, not looking too closely at his toes. He enters each session, as Wilfred Bion put it (borrowing from T.S. Eliot), "without memory or desire," counting on his discipline and skill to have been, like a dancer's or athlete's, subliminally encoded. Some analysts, more in need of a *Weltanschauung*, orient themselves to a simple principle, to wit: help the patient contact his feelings, give him a chance to grow in a nurturant atmosphere, show him how low his self-esteem is, or show him how destructive he is; virtually any permutation of human motive will suffice. More theoretically sophisticated analysts, dissatisfied with these simple manifestoes, find themselves embroiled in odd paradoxes. Often the therapist being theoretically clearer, or the patient the subject of special attention, makes the treatment more difficult. Every candidate in supervision will recognize this experience with his supervised patients. Patients will often recognize when a paper or presentation is incipient, or they will dream of supervisors, often placing age and sex quite accurately. Even excluding metapsychological considerations, thoughtful supervisors often recognize that they do not do, themselves, what they teach candidates to do; that there is a perceptual gap between what they do—their *praxis* of therapy—and their carefully conceived presentations of how it *should* be done.

Alas, theory and practice would appear irreconcilable. Theoretical clarity does not necessarily aid in therapy; it may be harmful. Clinical practice does not appear to derive from theory in any straightforward fashion. Operational limits make it impossible for therapists to stand sufficiently outside of their praxis to be able to formulate clearly what it is they do when they do it. Research is notoriously difficult in this area, since the very presence (or knowledge) of the observer changes the psychoanalytic frame and the interactions of all the participants. Moreover, one can only measure what one notices, and many of the crucial interactions in the psychoanalytic process are so subtle or so attenuated, extended over many sessions, that they confound observation. To quote Anna Freud again, "What is lost, finally, is what used to be considered the *sine qua non* in psycho-analytic thinking: the essential unity between clinical and theoretical thinking."[4]

I wish to advance the hypothesis that in spite of all this confusion there *is* a commonly held praxis of therapy. *All* psychoanalysts, regardless of doctrinaire convictions, follow essentially the same process; they all go about doing therapy in the same way.

Basically, the thesis is that Josef Breuer, and then Freud, fell upon a powerful therapeutic instrument, what Anna O., the first patient, called the "talking cure." The fallacy was the attribution of the power of this method to *what* was talked about, rather than the very process of talking. It must be remembered that the procedure was unique: a patient and a doctor sat and *talked,* and psychiatric symptoms were relieved without any laying on of hands. Why should talking be therapeutic? It must be, Freud reasoned, *what* was talked about. The patient came to learn something about himself that had been heretofore denied. The efficacy of therapy must, he reasoned, be dependent on the *content* of the therapy. It subsequently became clear that it was also dependent on the way it was talked about, Freud's signal discovery of resistance and transference. Nevertheless, content was at the core of the process, and the search for a theory of therapy that correlated content and process began and still continues, since, according to Khan, "it is an accepted fact in recent psychoanalytic discussions that an integrated theory of psychoanalytic technique, as yet, does not exist."[5]

But, if one examines the *context,* not content, of the insights, one sees a highly clarified and defined linguistic discourse. In a situation of great constraint—which limits and contains the anxiety of both participants and, consequently, their anxious claims on each other—they talk. They examine what is talked about, and they examine the context in which it is talked about: that is, who they are for each other. This intense dialogue, relatively isolated from mutual social claims, is unique in the secular western world and perhaps comparable only to the guru experience in the eastern world.

I am suggesting that the effectiveness of this procedure depended on Freud's unwitting application of a linguistic *algorithm*, a systematic series of steps for achieving an outcome. An algorithm, it must be noted, can work even if the theoretical underpinnings are wrong or irrelevant; ancient algorithms for making bronze, tin, even steel existed long before the onset of scientific metallurgies.

Freud's algorithm tapped into the deep structure of discourse, built into the human system—a part of cognitive programming that has nothing whatever to do with the conscious or unconscious but operates totally outside of awareness. When presented with problems, people are capable of very sophisticated cognitive processes that seem built-in and neither conceptualized nor contrived consciously. If this algorithm resonates to an inherent structure, then its effectiveness does not depend entirely on the truth or value of the material presented—that is, its content. Psychoanalysts must recognize that they are participating on a continuum of influence that is essentially amoral and that ranges from the propaganda of Dr. Goebbels on one end to the psychotherapeutic persuasions practiced deliberately, with honorable intent, by some group and family therapists—and often unwittingly by some psychoanalysts—at the other end. This is a vital caveat: psychoanalysts who believe their therapy "works" because of the superior Truth of what they say, rather than because they are utilizing a powerful tool of influence, are in danger of an evangelistic self-deception.

Presented with a valid and original therapeutic instrument, Freud stood at a crossroads. He had a method; he needed an explanation. For reasons that will be explicated in this book, he chose to apply the psychoanalytic algorithm to the world of fantasy. The child was seen as distorting reality because he *was* a child and lived, as children do, in a world of phantasmagoria; not because he was too inexperienced and too semiotically limited to grasp reality in its true complexity. *Thus, an irrevocable schism opened up between psychological reality as fantasy and psychological reality as mystified experience.*

We are left with the perplexing spectacle of psychoanalysts of interpersonal and intrapsychic persuasion sharing essentially the same algorithm: that is, going about doing psychoanalysis much the same way, and yet totally unreconciled about the goals of treatment and the definition of cure. From the interpersonal perspective, much that passes as cure in the intrapsychic literature smacks of what Erich Fromm called "reform." From the intrapsychic view, much of the interpersonal resolutions seem chaotic, unsettled, and indeterminate.

Recently there has been a very strong conviction, among some analysts, that we are drawing closer together, that a unified theory of psychoanalysis may be forthcoming, and that perhaps "object-relations" theory offers that messianic path. This loosely affiliated group of theories, to varying degrees, holds a commitment both to intrapsychic drive theory and to the significance of human relations, thus appearing to bridge the schism between the intransigencies of traditional psychoanalysis and interpersonal theory. Notwithstanding this possible theoretical rapprochement, there has been a decided ecumenical movement, among psychoanalysts in general, based on the undeniable reality that however we label it we all seem to be doing something in common. One hears erstwhile Freudians talking about the "self," a clearly interpersonal construct, and considering the significance of "real" early experience with mothering. One heard interpersonalists talking about "projective identification." The old eponymous party-line distinctions have become blurred: Sullivanians, Freudians, Frommians have lost their hard-edged distinctions. There are Sullivanians who now seem like closet Freudians and Freudians who appear wistfully more at ease with their apostatic colleagues than with their own institutional peers. No longer marching in close ranks on the Royal Road to the Unconscious, we seem to be milling at the crossroads; to be in that most literal sense of the word in crisis. But the real crisis in psychoanalysis does not lie in the unrealized relationship of practice to theory, if one can accept my premise that there is a shared praxis. The crisis lies in the relationship of praxis to *purpose.* The overlay of diverse theoretical positions does not significantly effect the algorithm of treatment but does lead to an insidious and dangerous discrepancy in the tacit goals of therapy, the concepts of therapeutic ends.

By examining what Freud discovered—the nature of the algorithm, how he utilized it, and how the metapsychology came to focus on distortion of experience—the gap between his development and the subsequent American pragmatic psychoanalytic movement may become evident. I will postulate that the algorithm is imbedded in *language,* not fantasy, and that the largely semiotic interpersonal psychoanalysis of Harry Stack Sullivan melds most easily into this model. The consequence for treatment methods and goals will be explored with particular emphasis on the politics of change and on the relationship between two versions of cure—*sincere* reform and *authentic* enrichment.

I will be making essentially two points: first, that all analysts tap into the same linguistic process regardless of their hermeneutics or explanatory systems. Psychoanalysis, like any art, is the exaltation of the ordinary. What psychoanalysts do is no more than a highly disciplined and scrupulously observed version of what occurs when people talk with each other. Its power resides in its link to the commonplace, rather than to some special esoteric meaning. Psychoanalysts, like magicians, may achieve their most genuine effects by unwittingly tapping into a natural structure of events, rather than by assiduous application of cherished rituals. The second point is that a radical split has occurred in the utilization of this method. Moreover, the split so transcends institutional borders that analysts have their own "borderline" problems, as I shall suggest with clinical material. Psychoanalysis, like Freud's Oedipus, confronts its destiny at a series of intercalated crossroads. I would claim that there are irrevocable and essentially irreconcilable choices to be made. A strong case will be made for the superior relevance of the interpersonal perspective. However, it must be allowed that this remains for psychoanalysis a very considerable bone of contention that will not be buried by my efforts.

There has been a revival of interest in Freud's historicity since the opening of the Freud archives in 1982. Many questions are being raised about his therapeutic directions, and an effort to disavow his direction without disavowing the process would be akin to, for once, throwing out the bath water and keeping the baby. It would extend the formulations of *The Fallacy of Understanding,* my first sortie into this area.[6] It would endorse a psychoanalytic inquiry rooted in the matrix of real experience—of both patient and therapist—in which a successful outcome of therapy would not be divesting oneself of infantile distortions but, rather, developing interpersonal competence based on semiotic skills that make it possible to distinguish the nuances of interaction. In this perspective, personal enrichment of self and of interpersonal competence is held to be synonymous with mental health. One hopes to enlarge the patient, not "shrink" him.

As in *The Fallacy of Understanding,* I have used essentially an essay form, which permits more sweeping generalizations, and less point-by-point documentation than academic writing traditionally entails. This may be an irritant to some readers and a relief to others. At any rate, it lends itself to my purpose, which is a perspectivistic overview of psychoanalysis in its time.

I think that very profound unconscious premises about the nature of reality pervade our conceptualizations, and that these premises are culture-bound and quite capable of shifting under us, without our awareness. Since, as I've suggested, psychoanalysts retain a considerable power to influence, regardless of the correctness of their theses, it behooves them to draw careful distinctions between persuasion and cure, between propaganda and self-realization. The analyst convinced of the immutable relevance of his position may find himself, like a penguin, drifting out to sea on a melting bed of premises.

CHAPTER 2

Freud's Choice:
Facts or Fiction

Once upon a time, I, Chuang Tsu,
dreamed I was a butterfly, flying happily
here and there. Suddenly I woke up and
I was indeed Chuang Tsu. Did Chuang
Tsu dream he was the butterfly, or did
the butterfly dream he was Chuang Tsu?
—G. FENG AND J. ENGLISH
Chuang Tsu: Inner Chapters

WE WOULD all agree that symbolization, in its divers manifestations (dreams, fantasies, the patient's representation of events, even language itself), mirrors actual events. But when there is distortion, when an evident gap exists between real events and their symbolic representation, does the distortion reflect an attempt to grapple with a poorly comprehended reality; or is the reality only a jumping-off point for an autonomous fantasy process, internally driven and motivated? Who dreams the dream? Does the dream perhaps dream the dreamer? My thesis is that precisely this issue lies at the core of a major psychoanalytic schism, one with profound and perhaps irreconcilable consequences for our understanding of the process of therapy and the very nature of change.

To be sure, at the core of every neurotic difficulty there is distortion; but distortion may be read as fantasy imposed on the present, or as an agonistic effort to grapple with bewildered experience. For the former, psychoanalysis exorcises the infantile; for the latter, it elucidates the uncomprehended.

Freud first took one path and then abruptly reversed direction. Whether he went another way or simply backed down the same road is open to some question, as I shall indicate. Sullivan, entering the psychoanalytic arena from an entirely different direction, also arrived at a crossroads. For both innovators, a major life crisis was ushered in by a prescient dream. Both, I claim, backed away from the radical extensions of their positions.

It is useful, before examining the commonly held algorithm of psychoanalysis, to review the historical development of Freud's ambiguity toward his own clinical material and towards his iconic myth, Sophocles' *Oedipus Rex*. It will then be possible to elaborate the implications of Freud's drive theory and to show how Sullivan's interpersonal psychoanalysis led in another direction.

There has been, as I indicated, a recent sharply focused critical inquiry into the psychohistorical aspects of Freud's life and writings. Although no doubt stimulated by Anna Freud's opening of the complete Freud-Wilhelm Fliess correspondence in 1982, it also reflects a subtle but inexorable shift in clinical perspective. The marvelous work *Freud: Living and Dying,* by Freud's physician and colleague Max Schur, was published in this country in 1972, and an expurgated version of the Fliess correspondence appeared earlier, in 1954.[1] Although the latter in particular attracted a certain amount of scholarly attention, the book was put out largely as an effort to polish an acknowledged and accredited thesis. Recent inquiries are far more insidious and revolutionary. They question the very basis of Freud's psychoanalysis, claiming that the entire metapsychological structure was a neurotic defense of Freud's against forbidden insights into his own life. As Marie Balmary put it, the theory is a defense against the "fault" of the father.[2]

Ordinarily, ad hominem attacks are viewed as having no great relevance. A theory presumably stands free of its creator. The present efforts to reconstruct Freud's life have a different purpose. They are launching an attack on the *theory* and its consequences for doing therapy. The historical reconstruction is, then, simultaneously a doctrinary repudiation and an attempt to salvage Freud by retracing his steps to the point where he presumably went awry. Freud must be reconstructed, reinterpreted, rehabilitated. Although this smacks of George Orwell's *1984,* the identity and integrity of the psychoanalytic movement depends on it. Without opposition or agreement to Freud, psychoanalysis ceases to exist.

It is commonly held that the great epiphany of psychoanalysis came about in 1897, when Freud's seduction/betrayal theory was discarded. Freud decided, to his great dismay, that his previously held idea that neurosis was caused by actual seduction by the caretaker or parent was untenable. He had previously written to Fliess that "in every case, the father, not excluding my own, had to be blamed as a pervert."[3] Via a quantum intellectual leap, he now reversed his original position. The seduction, he decided, was "fantasy." It was symbolic, and since external stimulation did not supply the necessary energy, the entire theory of an internal machinery "driven" or energized by an intrinsic libido emerged. Why did he not go in the other obvious direction, the one now held by interpersonalists and family therapists: namely, that the seductions were real, but not *literal?* Obviously, there are many more ways of seducing a child than by frank genital abuse. In his case examples, Freud had already touched on just such betrayals, such failures of what Erik Erikson was later to call *fidelity*. [4] Erikson's exegesis of the Dora case, delineating the blatant disloyalties of Dora's father and, indeed, of Freud, followed easily from Freud's own observations. The discrepancies were clearly waiting to be seen. Why did he not see them? Or, perhaps more to the point, why did he not *see* that he saw them?*

Marianne Krüll has suggested an interesting answer to that question in her book *Freud und Sein Vater.* † Krüll examines the critical years from 1885 to 1897, when Freud repudiated his seduction theory. Krüll, as I do, considers this point in Freud's theorizing not as the beginning of psychoanalysis but as a "major derailment." In October 1896, the year prior to his theoretical shift, Freud's father had taken ill and died. Freud, then forty, described the death of his eighty-one-year-old father as "the most upsetting loss in the life of a man." In May of 1897, when Freud was on the verge of expanding his seduction/betrayal theory, he was suddenly overcome with malaise and intellectual paralysis. Several months later, he jettisoned five years of work on the seduction theory. Krüll sees the key to Freud's decision in a dream he reported to Fliess, a dream he had the night after his father's funeral. In a letter dated October 1896, Freud reports that this dream occurred when he fell asleep at his barber's; he arrives "rather late" to the funeral home because he is delayed at the barber shop. In *The Interpretation of Dreams* the setting has become a railway station.[6] In the dream, he reads on a board the following message: "It is requested to close the eyes." Krüll believes that Freud explicitly had been on the brink of delineating dynamic family

---

*It is curious that a number of the revisionists have gone back literally to Freud's seduction theory, i.e., that children are seduced by adults. Karl Menninger wrote of his facilities for wayward girls, "75% of the girls we accept at the Villages have been molested in tender childhood by an adult. . . . why oh why couldn't Freud believe his own ears?" (*New York Times*, August 25, 1981)

†It has not been translated from the German as yet. I am working from a review by Sophie Freud Loewenstein, Freud's granddaughter.[5]

processes—mystification, betrayal, and exploitation—which would have compromised his relationship to his father.

There was indeed much mysterious to Freud in his father's history, including an unmentioned second wife (Freud's mother was his father, Jacob's, third wife), and the reasons for the family leaving Freiburg for Vienna when he was four. Some mystery or possible "scandal" causing the hasty departure was implied.[7] According to Balmary, Jacob not only had a second wife who was mysteriously expunged from family accounts, but Sigmund's birthplace records reflected that he was born eight months after his parents' marriage. This discrepancy in family accounts, according to Balmary, recurs repeatedly in Freud's analytic endeavors and in the patterning of his own life.

The claim that Freud stood his theoretical position on its head because of an injunction not to "see" his own father's behavior—that is, out of a wish not to confront his relationship with the now-dead father—may seem farfetched. But one may turn for further verification to the "specimen dream" of psychoanalysis, the Irma dream of 1895.[8] This is the dream of Irma's injection, about which in 1900 Freud wrote to Fliess, "Do you actually suppose that some day this house will have a marble plaque with the inscription: 'Here on July 24th, 1895, the mystery of dreams was revealed to Dr. Sigm. Freud?'"

In the dream Irma attends a reception given by the Freuds and complains to Freud of pains in her throat and stomach. Freud reproaches her for not accepting his "solution." He looks in her mouth and discovers a white leukoplakic patch and some curly structures modeled on the turbinal bones of the nose. There follows an elaborate exchange in which his friend "Otto" is held responsible for having given her an injection with a dirty syringe. The dream mechanism is described as Freud's annoyance with Otto's criticism of his, Freud's, cure and his wish for revenge. The dream, then, is a form of symbolic revenge: the disease is Otto's fault, not his. Charles Rycroft attempts in his book *The Innocence of Dreams* to anchor the dream in reality by pointing out the sexual connotation of the imagery and Freud's possible jealousy of Irma's attraction to the young and handsome Otto.[9] This interpretation would correspond to the actual circumstances surrounding the dream.

There is, however, a simply incredible story underlying all this. Schur, in his examination of the unpublished Fliess correspondence, presents the following events. Freud, as is known, had an intense attachment to Fliess, a Berlin ear, nose, and throat specialist, who had a theory that related sexual pathology to nasal anomalies. Freud was initially very taken with this view, which, as Sulloway points out, was not, in its context, considered a crank idea. There was among physicians of the time considerable interest in the correlation of nasal pathology and sexual disorders.[10] At any rate, Fliess performed some fairly draconian nose surgery to relieve emotional difficulties and had, in fact, done such surgery on Freud's nose.

Consider this: Freud had asked Fliess to operate on Emma (Irma), since his therapy with her was going slowly. Fliess did a major excision of her turbinate bone, inadvertently left a half-meter strip of iodoform gauze in the wound, and went home to Berlin. Upon later discovery and removal of the gauze by another surgeon, Emma hemorrhaged severely and went into shock. Freud, who was present, almost fainted at the odor and profuse bleeding and had to leave the room. Emma was extremely ill afterward and required several other surgical interventions. Freud blamed not Fliess but the second ENT man for the hemorrhage! Schur agrees that Freud was unable to blame his father-substitute, Fliess, although Schur did not have available some of the data later uncovered by Krüll.

Why, then, when Freud interpreted the dream, did he not

consider its obvious reality implications? Quite simply, the dream *says what happened,* and the intensity of the dream, and Freud's guilt, are quite appropriate to the stimulus. The symbolism leads to a real event: one need not postulate an energic source from within.

In other words, Freud deliberately decided to minimize the actual events that stimulated the dream and to treat it as though it were a symbolic construct around a minor event—Freud's wish not to be criticized. Freud says, "Look, what a brouhaha symbolism makes of a simple, very trivial event!" Much the same observation of dissimulation could be made about another of Freud's famous clinical studies, the Schreber case. Morton Schatzman has claimed that every one of Schreber's delusions could be related to an actual apparatus of his father, a well-known and widely-read educator.[11] Schreber's father had developed devices—literally, straitjackets and braces—to bend the child to his will. Freud knew of the father's many publications. Why would Freud not have seen what seems to us obvious symbolic representations of the real? Krüll would say that Freud could not "see" the real failure of the father figure and so made it a fantasy, something "all in his [Schreber's] head."

I must reemphasize a point made earlier: the consequences of believing that the dream dreams the person, that the fantasy is the patient's reality, is that real events are devalued, designified, and seen only as the grain of sand that starts the pearl-making process. All of Freud's cases support this point: what the parents really do is *not* important; only the fantasy elaborations count. It would seem, then, that psychoanalysis, historically at least, is based on a deception; conscious or unconscious, it remains what Jean-Paul Sartre called "Bad Faith".[12] One can see the present consequences of this position. Intrapsychic analysis has affirmed such a stance, and even the current literature is replete with clinical examples wherein the most blatant reality is ignored in pursuit of symbolization. Note this quote from Peter Giovacchini: "The psychoanalytic setting is so constructed that the reality of the surrounding culture does not operate as such: references to reality can be regarded as reflections of various mental operations of the analysand."[13] Along these same lines, Louise Kaplan says that "the passions of childhood, our appetites, dreads, longings, envies, jealousies, came into existence in connection with our infantile interpretations of an actual world populated by ordinary persons."[14]

I think this position is dead wrong. Freud, like his model Moses, made a wrong turn in the desert. The consequence is a therapy that emphasizes distortion and misunderstanding and that has as its cure the giving up of one's own idiosyncratic reality. It may appear at this point that I've set up a straw man; no one, you say, is *that* opaque or unaware of the importance of real events and misconstrued experience in the patient's life. It is true that most analysts give some lip service to the importance of actual experience, but a virtual chasm of difference opens when one examines detailed clinical data. Nowhere is this more evident than in the concept of "transference." If one believes in the relevance of concrete events in the patient's present life and history, then one must also believe in their relevance to the patient/therapist interaction. The interpersonal therapist must grapple with the *real* matrix of events and personalities in which every therapy is embedded. It is not a question of what the patient has projected "onto" or "into" the therapist, but of really *who* the therapist is and *what* he brings to the therapy encounter. There are profound assumptions about the therapy process that are the therapist's contributions to the mystification process.

Freud came upon a momentous discovery: the transformational nature of discourse; that is, that language, *sui generis*, had powerful therapeutic consequences. Rather than focusing on process qua process, he attempted to consolidate it as therapeutic device. When his first premise, that childhood seductions had occurred, proved unfounded, he reversed his field and postulated that the child's inflamed imagination invented seductions and assaults. This shift may be less substantive than it appeared; I would suggest that it is a polemical device, a way of salvaging intact the original thesis of force, counterforce, and subsequent distortion. For traditional psychoanalysis, behavior *is* conflict; between person and person, between drive and defense.

Freud used the Oedipus myth as a metaphor for justifying the universality of human behavior as conflict. It was a clever rhetorical device that anchored his theories in time and antiquity, appropriating the formidable prestige of classicism. There have been, of course, many critiques of Freud's cooptation of the Sophoclean drama. As I shall elaborate in the next chapter, there are aspects of the story and of Freud's lifetime fascination with it that point to a different road.

CHAPTER 3

The Oedipus Myth:
Conflict or Mystery

Who divined the famed riddle (of the
Sphinx) and was a man most mighty.
—SOPHOCLES
Oedipus Rex

THE EVIDENCE that Freud recanted his original seduction theory because of personal psychodynamics is persuasive, but the psychohistorical explanations proffered are considerably less convincing. We are to believe that Freud, retreating from the recognition of his father's "fault," jettisoned his original belief in "real" seductions in the child's life and contrived an intrapsychic theory of neurosis. The argument is that real events in Freud's life were hidden, buried, kept from his awareness, and that the requirement that these events be kept out of awareness led to his shift. "The perverse conduct of an adult is actually at the origins of the problems," as Balmary put it.[1] Freud was right the first time, it says: real traumas cause neurosis; Freud's shift of theory is an example par excellence of that mechanism. As Gregory Bateson said: "Epistemology is always and inevitably *personal*. The point of the probe is always in the heart of the explorer."[2]

But a family scandal—that is, Freud's father's hidden marriage and Freud's possibly out-of-wedlock conception—does not seem sufficient psychic trauma to account for his creative crisis and abrupt reversal of position. The attested trauma is not an event; it is an *omission*—Freud was not supposed to be aware of something that he knew about but which was presumably never spoken of. The trauma consists not in what happened, but in that it went unsaid. What "energized," "cathected" Freud's odd response to historical omissions? One must postulate conflict: on what grounds, then, since Jacob Freud was to all appearances a mild and affectionate man? One must postulate conflict based on fantasy leading to distortion. Q.E.D. To attribute to the events sufficient force to cause Freud's recantation requires, ironically enough, falling back on a post-Freudian explanation: namely, that some fantasy energizes the reversal. Thus, one has returned to an energic drive theory of neurosis. The implicit thesis is that Freud accepted the injunction not to see, not because the events were, in themselves, so traumatic, but because of a powerful oedipal submission to his father that was activated by his father's death.

The explanation falls back on what it sets out to discredit. It remains within the libido tautology and consequently lacks conviction.

In the letter to Fliess referred to in the previous chapter, Freud, before his recantation, referred to the seducer "in every case, including my own" as being the father. After his delineation of the fantasy thesis, Freud was even more committed to a mechanistic theory of conflict which required that the parents, particularly the mother, be viewed as *deis ex machina*, simply being there to initiate an inexorable mechanism, the Oedipus complex.

If one eschews instinct theory and approaches the matter from a more interpersonal perspective, it seems likely that the "secret" was bound into a social matrix of events, attitudes about events, and attitudes about revealing events, involving loyalties, the rhetoric of disclosure—who is permitted to know what—the entire matrix of social experience. What did Freud know? What did he not know? What did he know about what he was not supposed to know he knew?

I would claim that fantasies grow in the soil of omission: what is not known is imagined. What is half-known is embellished. Why was the secret "selectively inattended" (to use Sullivan's term)? We shall never know. Certainly Freud's preoccupation with Moses, another leader with ambiguous birth, his own strange ménage with his wife and her sister, would reflect a lifetime mulling of these issues. But the motivation is not fantasy per se, but half-truths, rooted in the ground of omitted information. From this perspective, neurotic distortion emerges from the relationship between what is done and what is *said* about what is done.

As for the dream of Irma's injection, there are then three possibilities. First, that Freud unconsciously repressed his knowledge of Fliess's fault, the position held by Schur, Greenberg and Perlman, and Balmary.[3] It is consistent with oedipal theory to see his defense of Fliess in the Irma incident as a "dynamic," but a second position suggests a conflict of values—loyalty to a friend and colleague versus medical truth. We do know that Freud's father fostered and admired Sigmund's loyalty. "My Sigmund's little toe is cleverer than my head, but he would never dare to contradict me."[4] Fliess was notoriously short-tempered. Was Freud perhaps simply afraid of him? We do not, after all, know his inner feelings. We have only a letter to Fliess. Perhaps Freud's reaction to Fliess's bungle did not arise from a specific dynamic but from a more pervasive problem with issues of criticism, dissent, and disloyalty. It is clear that Freud, throughout his career, had grave difficulties with these issues, either avoiding confrontation until an open rift developed or, as in the case of Jung's defection, developing fainting spells. Thus, one might claim that out of conscious loyalty to Fliess and out of fear of damaging Fliess's reputation, he deliberately exculpated any data that would point to the surgery—a view held by Adam Kuper and Alan Stone.[5] No one advances the third possibility, a rather more unsavory one—that he was promulgating, with ferocious ambition, a theoretical position that would have been, at the very least, weakened by the background facts. Schur quotes Freud, in a letter to Fliess, as indicating that he could tailor his dreams "to order."[6] Thus, Fliess's culpability could have been repressed, inattended, or simply dissimulated.

We have virtually none of the data a contemporary psychoanalyst, of any persuasion, would consider necessary to an informed interpretation of Freud's motives. A great veil of silence has been drawn around the myth of the Hero. Any inquiry requiring an archeological approach: shards of letters, Freud's dreams, and his interest in mushrooms, Moses, and da Vinci. Freud has imposed on us his method and his myth. Twice, in 1882 and again in 1907, he destroyed personal papers, deliberately obscuring any autobiographical data that would reveal him. In 1885, the heroic self-revealer of dreams wrote to his fiancée:

> I certainly had accumulated some scribblings. But that stuff settles around me *like sand drifts around the sphinx* [emphasis added]; soon nothing but my nostrils would have been visible above the paper. I couldn't have matured or died without worrying about who would get hold of those old papers. . . . As for my biographers, let them worry, we have no desire to make it too easy for them. Each one of them will be right in his opinion of "The Development of the Hero" and I am already looking forward to seeing them go astray.[7]

Like the sphinx whose silence guards the tombs of the pharaohs, Freud placed himself across his own path and has left us not, as he wished, with a heroic conflict, but rather with a mystery.

The sphinx is a recurrent theme in Freud's writings. It sat prominent among the bibelots on his desk, was depicted in a painting in his office, and was a central theme in his writings. Why did Freud fantasy, according to Ernest Jones's account, that one day in the Hall of Fame his bust would bear the very inscription from Sophocles quoted at the beginning of this chapter? In 1906, his followers had a medallion struck as a birthday surprise and, with unconscious prescience, picked Freud's dreamed-of inscription. When Freud read the quote, he became "pale and agitated and in a strangled voice demanded to know who had thought of it."[8] Why would Freud assign himself Oedipus' dreadful destiny?

What is the Sphinx, that Cairo tourist attraction, doing, anyway, crouched on the road to Thebes, asking a puerile nursery riddle and then strangling anyone unable to answer it? According to Robert Graves, the myth of the Sphinx derived from an icon showing the winged moon goddess of Thebes.* Her composite body—woman, lion, and serpent—represented the two parts of the Theban year, waxing and waning moons. In the early mother-worship days, before the coming of the Olympian paternalistic gods, the new king offered his devotions to the moon goddess before marrying her priestess, the queen. The riddle, which the Sphinx had learned from the muses, represented a pictograph of an infant, a warrior, and an old man—all ages of man—each of whom is paying homage to the different aspects of the triple-goddess. Graves asks:

*One notes that sphincter is from the same Greek root as sphinx; namely, to squeeze or strangle. To limit poetic license, I must also confess that the Egyptian sphinx was, according to Herodotus, *androsphinx*, or male sphinx. The female sphinx is probably Ethiopian.[9]

"Was Oedipus a thirteenth-century invader of Thebes, who suppressed the old Minoan cult of the Goddess and reformed the calendar? Under the old system the new King, a foreigner, had theoretically been a son of the old King whom he killed and whose widow he married—a custom that the patriarchal invaders misrepresented as parricide and incest.[10]

Graves goes on to point out, somewhat waspishly, that although Plutarch records that the hippopotamus "murdered his sire and forced his dam," he would "never have suggested that every man has a hippopotamus complex." Nor, one might add, would he suggest that Sisyphus had a love-hate relationship with a rock.

There are, then, two distinct aspects to the Oedipus myth: the killing of Laius at the crossroads of Phocis and the defeat of the Sphinx. The former is patricide and the latter, matricidal. Graves said that the myths dealt with the incompatibility of serving the ancient matriarchal goddesses and the newer Aryan patriarchal Olympians. This incompatibility runs through the Sophoclean trilogy. The Oracle at Delphi that joins Laius and Oedipus (Laius was on his way to consult the Oracle about the Sphinx's depredations, and Oedipus was returning from the shrine) was a war spoil of Apollo, who killed the sacred python of the matriarchal goddess and appropriated her priestess (the Oracle). At his death, in the final play of the Sophoclean trilogy, Oedipus makes his peace with the Furies, representatives of the Ancient Mother at Colonus.

Moreover, it is the defeat of the Sphinx that makes Oedipus (and Freud) a Hero, the defender of Thebes.* He is made king for that feat, not for the killing of Laius, the present king. The myth, then, concerns the *conflict* of father-son and the *mystery* of mother-son. Note that Oedipus defeats the Sphinx through

---

*Hero is from the Indo-European root *ser,* to protect.

cleverness, not brawn. What is the trick to answering the riddle? It requires a capacity for analogy, for seeing connections heretofore not evident, but obvious once seen.

Psychoanalysts must certainly recognize in that the similarity to their process. This is of extraordinary interest. Oedipus does not triumph in battle, like the mythic Heroes. He does not, like Perseus, slay the Gorgon. The male principle in these myths is to conquer by force. Unlike Alexander, who does not bother to untangle the gordian knot but draws his sword and cuts it, Oedipus does not conquer; he deciphers. The Sphinx throws herself to her death. The monster is not overthrown by a blustering Hero, half-human, half-god, and invincible, but by Mother's clever little boy. The tongue becomes mightier than the sword.*

Freud saw himself as the hero who conquered neurosis by deciphering its code. The fascination of Oedipus was that he revealed the mysteries of the Earth Mother, putting light and knowledge in their place and then paying the price. For "where Id was, there shall Ego be," one might read "where mystery was, there shall clarity be." The relation between mother-worship and "mystery" is not incidental, since the Eleusinian mysteries were ceremonies of the early Mother goddesses and were forbidden to men on threat of death. The initiate priestesses were *mystes,* bound to silence. "Mystery," one notes, is from the Greek *myein, to close the eyes! Vide* Freud's dream: "It is required to close the eyes" may refer at least as much to respecting mystery as to denying castration.

To repeat the central question: why did Freud, after identifying himself with a hero of language, after devising a therapeutic device that operates through language, recant? To say that the unknown was so horrible is to fall back on Instinct theory;

---

*Much the same hegemony exists in primates, where the alpha male is often not the most powerful male but the offspring of the dominant female.

ordinary events are distorted out of all proportion by the imagination of the child. How did Jacob Freud's possibly unsavory secret become an awesome mystery?

If one sees behavior as conflict, then one must postulate a struggle between Freud and his father. Jacob's death then releases Freud to make his great leap forward. But perhaps Freud relinquished the seduction theory because it was patently untenable. He did not easily discard it, his first claim to fame as the discoverer of psychoanalysis. If the premise was wrong, was the entire enterprise? Perhaps his father's death released him, in some way, to *give up* an impossible stance. The reversal, at least, promised complexity and uncertainty.

Certainly Freud must have known that there was something he was not supposed to know, some mystery, or there would be no issue at all. Nor is the secret, in itself, really so dreadful. Not knowing, and not having the social sophistication to grasp the nuances of what he does know, the child fantasies and elaborates his scanty clues. The child overhears, inquires, and Mother says darkly, "Never mind! It's not for little ears." Freud was the little boy who wanted to decipher Mother's secret. A child does not fear to ask because he is afraid of the answer but because he will not be answered; he will be told, "you are too young to understand." Perhaps psychoanalysis is a field of endeavor that appeals to "old heads," preternaturally mature children who wish to prove that they are worthy of confidences.

The Oedipus myth grappled with an elusive, mysterious reality. *It was an attempt to come to grips with real events through the use of imagery.* For Freud, it was imagery run wild, dominating and directing its creator. For Freud, imagery or symbolism is not an effort to connect people to a poorly apprehended and understood outside world, but rather creates an inner reality that is at odds with the real world and that compromises a person's capacity to see things as they really are. Whether due to personal blind spots, failure of an adequate paradigmatic base, or philosophical predilection, Freud did not complete the shift. To have entertained an interpersonal field would have been to embrace *not-knowing,* mystery; to be the real child, not the idealized parent. For the interpersonal field offers only an expansion of awareness, an enrichment of pattern, not the satisfying linear explanations of intrapsychic drive theory.

CHAPTER 4

Psychological Process:
Dynamics or Semiotics

No one has grave difficulties in living if
he has a very good grasp of what is
happening to him.

—H.S. SULLIVAN

ANY TRAVELER knows the feeling of dislocation and helplessness that comes with being in a land where one understands
the language imperfectly, does not know the customs or mores,
reads intentions poorly, and finds that the accouterments of
one's status at home are either missing or a matter of indiffer-
ence to the natives. In Germany, not smiling on introduction
implies mannerliness; in Japan, smiling may imply the opposite. No one knows this feeling of being Heinlein's "stranger
in a strange land" better than children. That is why, in the
extensive literature of children from Lewis Carroll's Alice to
aliens from other worlds or dimensions, it is always the children
these strange creatures engage. In *Wonderland* and *Looking
Glass*-land Alice struggles with all the bewildering paradoxes
of logic, syntax, semantics, custom, and intention experienced
by every child in the adult's world. As I've suggested, it was
not so different in the world of Oedipus. One could do the

right thing and be punished; one could be used wantonly in some internecine struggle of the gods. Tragedy is the gap between man's aspiration and the gods' arbitrariness. Hubris was willfulness in the face of this tragic inconstancy.

Let us consider four-year-old William playing with his Uncle George. Uncle George wrestles him to the floor and pins him firmly. The little boy tries to escape, stops smiling, begins to look dismayed, bursts into tears. Uncle George lets him up, calling him a sissy. An observer might note an odd glitter in Uncle George's eye. William is trying to master a complex interpersonal play; he is either a bad sport or he is being abused by his uncle. To make that distinction requires the development of *semiotic skill*; that is, skill in the entire range of symbolic exchanges. He must know custom; distinguish such rhetorical devices as irony, teasing, satire, and sarcasm; read nonverbal cues. As a further complication, semiotic messages may be, not mystified, inasmuch as that implies a purposeful process, but simply confused. The uncle may be teasing—deliberately misrepresenting the message—or he may honestly believe that he is playing with the child. In this sense he is promulgating and passing on his own confusion about levels of abstraction and metamessage.

It is a psychoanalytic truism that a man has premature ejaculations because he is hostile to women or afraid of castration. However, one notes that the extensive verbal and nonverbal discourse of sex seems to be beyond his comprehension. He does not know what he feels or what to feel; he is not aware of the messages from the woman—courting cures, expression, movement, smell, skin and muscle tone and color changes, lubrication, breathing. He cannot tell when she is enjoying, when she is pretending. He does not expect, in Hegel's famous phrase, to be the "object of her desire." He wishes only to perform and get it over with.

The number of frigid or impotent persons who have discovered sexual lust and performance with a new partner, one who moves and breathes and responds, are legion. Does the rage cause the impotence or does the impotence cause the rage? The cause of rage may be, not unconscious fantasy, but helplessness. Dependency results from helplessness, and helplessness comes from semiotic incompetence.

Psychological difficulties arise because of difficulty in sorting out the nuances of social experience, especially as it is mediated through language. Four-year-old William and the hapless lover are both mystified by their experience. I am claiming that mystification is not a secondary dissociation or fragmentation covered by anxiety, but a failure in a primary, vital skill. From this perspective, neurotic difficulties in living arise from *semiotic incompetence* rather than poorly integrated internal drives.

Semiotics, first defined and named by C.S. Peirce, the American philosopher, refers to "the transmission of signals, signs, signifiers, and symbols in any communication system whatever."[1] In the hierarchical ordering there is speech, then the intricate machinery for processing speech (language), and finally a more extensive system of coded communication that involves speech, nonverbal cueings, and most important, the cultural and social context of communication—what Charles Morris called the "pragmatics" of communication.[2]

Listen to this sentence: "You can't float a rock on borscht." Watch your mind scurry for meaning. First, it immediately begins to search for associative clusters, metonymic or contiguous meanings. Second, it wonders about the setting of the remark. And then, third, it wonders what is the name of the game. Borscht . . . Russian soup . . . Roumanian Jewish beet borscht (with sour cream) . . . Russian borscht (a very heavy, cabbage-and-meat hot soup) . . . rocks don't float . . . does a potato? Is it a pithy proverb told by one's Russian grandmother, is it a last line of a poem by Pasternak, is it from Ivan Turgenev, is it said by a schizophrenic, is it *intended* to be nonsense, is it a coded message, or is it, as in Jerzy Kosinski's novel *Being There*, nonsense being read as profound meaning by an audience?

Meaning, it is clear, is context-dependent. But context is elusive. If I tell you it is from a Russian novel, I still might be teasing you, pulling your leg, being contemptuous or even antisemitic. So, it depends on who is talking to whom, in what setting, and what communicational mode (irony, sarcasm, humor) is being used. To use another example: the noted psychologist Jerome Bruner, in discussing the development of just such skills in children, suggested that the child must learn that "Would you be so kind as to pass the salt?" is not an inquiry into his capacity for compassion.[3] This is a matter of semantics. But there is another pragmatic level; in this society, people do not use that degree of archaic formality unless they are furious! Any contemporary person, so addressed, would understand instantly that anger is implied.

Getting the message depends, then, on grasping these nuances. This is obviously very complicated and requires the development of considerable semiotic skills. Much of childhood is spent learning to focus these complex semiotic messages with their layers of metacommunication. From this radical interpersonal perspective, psychoanalysis becomes a communication between two real people engaging in a real way out of their own experience and personality. This engagement occurs through language and involves a series of communications and metacommunications; that is, communications about communications. Thus, as the patient talks, it is to the therapist, who selectively hears, decides what to respond to. There can be no response without selection. The therapist, in responding, behaves with the patient according to what they discuss. What is talked about is simultaneously played out between them.

There is no issue of "distortion" or of discovering what the truth is or of arriving at some distinction between real and unreal, none of those interpretive distinctions so integral to the classical format.

Every interpersonal exchange depends on levels of metacommunications in spoken language, on nonverbal cues, and on knowledge of the pragmatics, the social and cultural matrix in which the exchange takes place. This is clearly no simple matter and is never entirely mastered.

Nor are semiotic skills uniquely human. We are learning from ethological studies that animals have intricate rituals that are socially learned, not instinctive. For example, in the case of wild horses, the mare does not go to the most powerful stallion. She does not, as we have been led to believe, stand by demurely waiting to see who will win her. A successful stallion must court her, nibble her ear, and proceed through a series of exploratory approaches. Some stallions never master the style, get resoundingly kicked for their troubles, and do not mate, regardless of their fine coats or fighting prowess. With horses or apes or at singles bars, one must learn the rules of the game, and the rules are complicated indeed. Children think that when they become adults they will totally understand; adults understand that there are no adults.

Freud's child is alone in the woods at night, driven by primitive impulse, frightened of an animistic universe, imagined threats, and dangers. For Freud, fantasy fires anxiety; for Sullivan, anxiety, an empathic failure, fires fantasy—but it seems possible that anxiety is not only a primitive breakthrough of defenses but a complex social response *sui generis*. One may be overwhelmed or anxious or frightened because one thinks one should *not* be. This has long been known to military psychologists; the soldier most likely to break under fire is the one who believes a brave man is not frightened. Similarly, childhood anxiety becomes uncontained when the child thinks the parent is immune to his fears. The failure of empathy may be not only that the parent communicates anxiety contagiously but that he does not; and the child, isolated in his fear, has no social mechanism for coming to terms with it. The child who has discovered death and is afraid to sleep tells Daddy, who laughs and reassures him. Is he, then, the only one frightened? Fear and anxiety have their own metacommunications; one must learn to enjoy being frightened by ghost stories, to play at anxiety.

I would prefer the view of the child as a small person trying to find his way in a country of almost insurmountable complexity. It is evident that this view of relationships comes as much from anthropology, sociology, and linguistics as it does from medical psychiatry. As Bruner put it:

> The process of learning how to negotiate communicatively is the very process by which one enters the culture—initially the microculture of the family, and eventually the constituted world of the culture as a whole. And, moreover, it is in the act of relating oneself to others through the process of communication that the self is formed in a fashion to relate to the demands of one's culture. . . . it is in the negotiation of intended meaning that the self is formed.[4]

Language skills and the self are coterminous developments.

CHAPTER 5

The Symptom as Meaning:

Intrapsychic vs.

Interpersonal Perspectives

When the devil seals a contract, he takes,
as a token of the soul, something
insignificant, perhaps a tiny, almost
invisible piece of the nose . . .
—A folk tale

AS KARL MENNINGER has pointed out, Freud never devoted a book to technique, although "It may be this—the creation of an instrument of investigation—that will ultimately rank as his most important single contribution."[1] As I have indicated, for reasons of cultural and personal import Freud focused his attention on the development of a metapsychology, biologically and energically based. The traditional metapsychological perspectives—dynamic, genetic, topographic, structural, adaptive, and economic—essentially are simply different metaphors for the same energic mechanical paradigm. Some later theoretical developments, as Schafer put it, "may be subsumed under one or more of the traditional metapsychological points of view, while others, though couched in metapsychological language, may be shown to require the development of alternative theoretical language."[2] It is presumed that defenses contain, modify, and distort instinctual forces. Infantile sexuality is central to this thesis. The child must deal with powerful, uncivilized impulses. It is the function of his own defenses, his family, and society to contain and modulate them. Thus, it is understood that the little girl sitting on her daddy's lap is having anxiety because of her sexual feelings. If Daddy tickles her, this is a stimulating real event that may imbalance her controls but is not central to the theory.

From the interpersonal perspective, the sexual impulses of the child are not denied, but they are not the source of the problem. The child will become anxious if the father is anxious. Anxiety for Sullivan is an interpersonal event, a disruption in empathy. The father will become anxious if he is frightened by the child's feeling or his own seductiveness. Some obfuscation of this exchange will then occur. For example, the little girl wiggles on Daddy's lap. He suddenly becomes irritated and says, "Get off my lap if you can't sit still! Why must you jump around so!" The child is hurt but also mystified.

This is to some extent an oversimplification of both positions. Freudian psychoanalysts could claim with justice that they have gone far beyond this early formulation. But, I would claim that this very basic bifurcation in perception and purpose still lurks under the later, more sophisticated and ecumenical developments of psychoanalysis.

It might be argued, what difference does this difference make? Both sides of this alleged schism agree to the basic psychoanalytic algorithm. Both sides agree that family and society work to mold and contain the emergent child. Perhaps it is a chicken-and-egg question: does the child's fantasy lead to a distortion of the real event or does the real event lead to a distortion of the child's experience and, hence, a fantasy. Does it matter?

For the intrapsychic position, the enemy is within. For the interpersonalist, the enemy is without. From this latter perspective, the patient learns that his perceptions are shaped *in* interaction with others—not, you will note, *by* the reactions of others. The patient is not a passive victim. But he is being indoctrinated into a world where people act to maintain their own social stability. To this end, *semiotics*, not merely language, is the requisite skill, and to develop that skill a great deal of unambiguous experience is necessary. The child who lives in Sullivan's *parataxic* mode does not yet understand the relationship of events. He can grasp the issue of causality in the world only as it is told to him. To develop the *syntaxic* mode, he must order the world, put events in proper perspective. (Patrick Mullahy has the clearest definition of Sullivan's "horrendous" Greek trilogy of prototaxic, parataxic, and syntaxic. As the root suggests, the child learns reality as it is organized and ordered in language.)[3] This is a learned skill and a social one. Our patients are disabled not by their drives or inadequate defenses but, rather, by an inability to read and interpret the world, to grasp nuance, and to operate with sufficient skill to affect the people around them.

Perhaps a clinical vignette will help illustrate the difference. The patient is a twenty-eight-year-old man, a physician. He is a very attractive, cultivated man with impeccable academic credentials and flawless "Ivy League" manners. Neither his name nor his chiseled features would suggest that he is from a middle-class Jewish background. Both the name and the features have been altered: the former legally by his parents, and the latter surgically by him. It is of note that the rhinoplasty took place at age thirteen with the encouragement and cooperation of his parents, particularly his mother.

He is perfectly willing to be identified as Jewish, but his rhinoplasty is the most shameful secret of his life. He has never been able to reveal it to a lover or friend. His anguish approaches a state of idée fixe although he seems otherwise a reasonable and successful man. He is not disabled in social or professional functioning, although, of course, his secret acts as a barrier (or excuse for avoidance) of intimacy. The piece of his nose has been, for him, indeed a contract for his soul.

It's a silly enough problem. Is it simply false pride, arrogance, narcissism? If so, we know something about his character structure. Perhaps he is a "Portnoy," a narcissistic character, his self-esteem unable to tolerate this small flaw. Or, perhaps it is a small symptom with deep and malignant roots. It might signify his lack of authenticity, his tragic flaw revealed. Or, perhaps it signifies castration anxiety, either literally conceived or in the more abstract guise of a displaced doubt about his sexual attractiveness and penile competence. He does clearly feel mutilated and reduced.

Clinical case conferences have a field day with this kind of neat, extruded symptom. One will hear from colleagues a wide variety of what, if you will forgive a pun, one might call nosological assessments. In another, less professional milieu they would sound suspiciously like value judgments. On such occasions the depth of the analyst's religious convictions and the length of *his* nose often take precedence over metapsychological considerations. Or, more blatantly put, metapsychological and diagnostic considerations lend themselves rather facilely to personal prejudices.

At any rate, in therapy all efforts to engage the fantasy that underlay this man's inordinate distress were unavailing. On one occasion, he was again obsessing about whether he could bring himself to tell his fiancée his secret. The usual circular inquiry resulted. He then quite casually mentioned that he would need to change an appointment later in the week. He did not volunteer the reason, although it was not uncommon for him to rearrange hours to meet his hospital schedule. Nevertheless, the therapist inquired and was informed, again casually, that he was entering a hospital overnight to have some minor surgery done—a correction for a deviated septum in his nose. Why hadn't he mentioned it? It hadn't seemed important.

The therapist suddenly remembered a childhood occurrence the patient had reported a few sessions back. He had been accosted on his way home from school by a boy who threatened him with a knife. He had talked his way out of trouble, rather cleverly, but on his return home did not mention the incident to either parent. Why? He was not sure; they could be counted upon to respond reasonably and appropriately. His mother, particularly, had always been concerned and solicitous in a way that he somehow could never appreciate, although he did not understand why.

When the patient now revealed that he was to undergo surgery, the therapist made some vague sympathetic gesture, although post hoc he wondered why, since he was rather irritated with the patient's withholding information about the much-celebrated nose. On the other hand, the operation was really a very simple procedure. Why should the therapist feel offended at the exclusion?

At this point it occurred to the therapist that he had never thought to wonder why the patient felt obliged to tell his terrible secret, whatever its origins. Granted that it *was* an absurd concern; wasn't it his business whether or not to talk about it with others? Does intimacy depend on total revelation? Clearly, the patient felt that his relationship with another person would be irrevocably contaminated by withholding. Surely, though, it would have been a far more parsimonious solution for him simply to decide that, crazy or not, those were his feelings and he would keep them to himself. The patient was initially shocked and then intrigued when presented with this novel possibility.

One notes that the field of inquiry has shifted here from the meaning of the symptom to him as a solipsistic experience to the meaning of the symptom as a social event. Privacy, it developed, was not considered a manifest virtue in his family. Honesty and openness were encouraged. Secrecy or secretiveness were frowned upon and when he was "open" and revealed his feelings to his mother, she would respond empathetically and with concern. This was as true of his angry feelings as of any others. She always knew just how he felt and shared his distress. When he was upset about his appearance, she rushed him to the plastic surgeon. So, as in fairy tales, where the reward given by the magic helper is always much more than the recipient bargained for, the patient, like King Midas, got his wish. He was one of those unfortunate children of liberated and insightful parents who was doomed never to be misunderstood.

How could a child resent a parent who wanted to know everything and was sympathetic, concerned, and helpful? How could a child distinguish a symbiotic cannibalizing of his feelings from legitimate concern? To do so requires a very high degree of interpersonal skill and perceptiveness. Alice Miller has described this childhood dilemma with great sensitivity in her book *Prisoners of Childhood.* Coming from an object-relationship viewpoint, following the work of Donald Winnicott, Mahler, and Kohut, she says:

The child has a primary need to be regarded and respected as the person he really is at any given time, and as the center—the central actor—in his own activity.[4]

It has been said that masturbation is the child's first autonomous activity, the first self-gratification possible without the parent's participation. It may be that later, in preadolescence, lying and withholding are necessary developmental skills, protecting a precariously balanced sense of self until the adolescent (and postadolescent) develops semiotic skills that permit him to distinguish between authentic response and spurious concern. I suspect that trust in others (not that elusive infantile benediction, "basic trust," which is supposed to make the child forever-after trusting) is lost in preadolescence and recaptured as the child learns the extremely subtle variations in nuance of play: teasing, hurting, sarcasm, affectionate "ragging," irony. These are the exercises for the development of semiotic competence, as will be elaborated later.

Much of what has been described as "narcissism," a psychoanalytic rubric, can be equally subsumed under a semantic heading of sentimentality. Sentimentality can be defined as an investment in emotion as an experience, rather than as a transaction. The sentimentalist wishes to *feel* loving, to experience himself as a loving person, rather than to love someone. It is love in the intransitive state. The sentimental person appears warm, concerned, loving. How does the child distinguish between being a recipient of the other's caring and a bystander? It is very difficult. One can grow up in a family where the parents are sustainedly concerned, friendly, democratic; where the adolescent turmoils and dissensions never take place; and yet, the child is left with a vague gnawing dissatisfaction, a feeling, could he put it into words, of having been unengaged, neglected. A parent may avoid the child's anger, not out of fear of aggression—a dynamic explanation—but because he does not wish his "feeling good" disrupted. As Oscar Wilde put it, a sentimentalist is simply one who desires to have the luxury of an emotion without paying for it.

It is the thesis of this book that people do not run into difficulty because terrible things were done to them, or because
they distort ordinary experience into terror, but because they
are tangled in an elusive semiotic web of omissions, simula-
crums, and misrepresentations. The problem with narcissism
is not so much that it is depriving, which it certainly is, but
that it is confusing. A deprived child can, often does, turn else-
where—to a sibling, to the other parent, to a friend's parent.
But the confused child stays put, wondering why the love does
not satisfy.

Thus, a patient begins a session by describing a play he saw
in which a woman was untouched by life until an angry lover
slashed her face. It was her first marking by experience. He
then goes on to report a dream of two parts. In the first he
is going skiing and an attendant is helping him into a device,
a chairlift. But it requires assuming a rather contorted position.
In the second part, there is a small household idol, a demon
of some sort. It is being repaired by a blacksmith. As it is put
in the flames, it gets larger and larger, breaks loose, and consumes the countryside, eating everything in its way. This is
truly an ecumenical dream; it will delight the souls of analysts
from Freudian to Jungian to interpersonalist. One need only
add that the therapist is an avid skier. We would all agree that
the dream is "transferential"—that it refers, on one hand, to
the therapist's overcontrolling and binding the patient like
Schreber's father in Freud's famous case; and, in the second
part, to the patient's getting out of hand and destroying everything in sight. Is it fear of his oral aggression? What of its
mythic imagery? There is Vulcan and his forge; Zipa, the
mythical Tibetan monster who consumes everything in the
world and finally himself; there is the bed of Procrustes. There
is also a more humanistic explanation: namely, that the patient
is being pressured into conformity; that the parents are afraid

of his daemon, in Greek mythology a deified hero, or attendant spirit. Perhaps these are only different metaphors for the polarity of excessive constraint and excessive release.

But one may note, in both instances the patient goes trustingly to a helpful and presumably expert authority; both helpers, lift attendant and blacksmith, are impersonal experts. Each time, the results are less than desirable, but not from hostile intent. How does this "idolized" child come into touch with himself? How does one focus his consuming needs? Is it through interpretation, through transferential analysis? What of the countertransference? Can one label it countertransference if the therapist has never disliked this man who is unfailingly attractive, intelligent, and decent? Is it worth noting that he never makes the therapist feel stupid, unpleasant, or unlikable? Is it countertransference if one doesn't have a countertransference?* Perhaps the key to therapy is for the therapist to experience the patient in some real way, even if with contempt, disdain, or total boredom. The consuming demon may be considered his drives, his emergent power, or his interpersonal experience of never being impinged upon by others. In this last sense, endless expansion takes place in a vacuum. Does he need to contain his drives or to develop relationships with people who will engage him, impinge on him, contain him?

From this perspective, consuming aggression or hunger is not a consequence of untrammeled drive but of interpersonal experience that fails to feed or fails to establish limits to the patient's demands. In ordinary living, as in politics, power perverts. Safety and decency lie in the interpersonal matrix, not in an internalized superego. Surely the last forty years of world atrocities should have taught us that. One

*See Laurence Epstein for discussion of hate in the countertransference.[5]

must learn to distinguish between authentic engagement and sentimental bonhomie.

One could say that if the patient surrenders his last (and only) secret, he belongs totally to the other person. In principle he has no objection to that: he believes that state of oceanic "good boy" feeling to be coterminous with love. It is the demystification of his experience of trust, intimacy, and the authenticity of other people's response to him that makes it possible to drop the symptom. Interestingly, it is not lost; it simply stops being important. He learns that whatever its meaning and cause, it is no one's business but his. Besides, the woman's response is no validating indication of her care or concern. She could be amused, caring, or think him a jackass in this particular department. She might, or might not, reveal or even know her feelings in this matter. None of this really bears on her capacity for loving him, or for deceiving him.

Like all clinical vignettes, this one is both overly si:nplified and yet full of implicit possibilities. Nevertheless, if one sees the symptom as an expression of an interpersonal mystification rather than an intrapsychic fantasy imposed on reality, it emerges that the patient is upset because he cannot sort out the implications of his behavior. The focus of treatment becomes the elucidation of his experience with his mother in the historical past, his experience with women in the present, and with the therapist in the final common pathway, the therapist-patient relationship, loosely referred to as the transference. The therapist's contributions to this exchange are vital data that he must monitor, if not necessarily report to the patient.

The therapist, following the patient's flow of presentation and monitoring his own participation, hears the metaphor as *privacy and intimacy*. One notes I did not say that the metaphor *is* privacy. Metaphor is a carrying-over (etymologically) and is, by definition, perspectivistically infinite. The therapist did not hear this metaphor until it emerged in his relationship with the patient via the latter's "acting-out" of not telling about his new, reenacted nose surgery. The therapist interprets; that is, he points out the correlation, connects it with the incident with the mother (the therapist's association, but the patient's report). As will be elaborated later, he plays out, or in Ludwig Eidelberg's phrase, "acts-in" a dimension of his interpretation.[6] He says, in essence, "One doesn't have to see things that way. Secrets are possible. I am indicating clearly that I approve of that." Surely, this is directing the patient, or, at best, claiming to provide a corrective emotional experience. Yet it is done deliberately, because it commits the therapist to a confrontation with the problem the patient is having. It is all very well for the patient to know that he has difficulties with self-determination, but it is paradoxical to tell him that the problem shouldn't exist in therapy and *here* he must feel free to tell all and to trust the therapist who, presumably, can be counted upon to monitor and control his participation. Even if the therapist is trustworthy (therapists can be ethical and well-intended; that does not make them trustworthy), can the patient count on this benevolence from the rest of the world?

There is a much-quoted case of Sullivan's wherein he sees in consultation a young man who has been rapidly sinking into a schizophrenic decompensation.[7] On inquiry, Sullivan notes that the patient's parents are described as being quite perfect, beyond reproach, although they have obviously stifled every move towards independence the young man has attempted. Sullivan says to himself, "Oh yeah, it doesn't sound so good to me. It doesn't make sense. Maybe you've overlooked something." Does he say that to the patient? No way! What he does say is, "I have a vague feeling that some people might doubt the utility to you of the care with which your parents, and par-

ticularly your mother, saw to it that you didn't learn to dance."
Then Sullivan reports, "I was delighted to see the schizophrenic young man give me a sharp look." This exchange, which
I think is in language and style worthy of a Baker Street Regu-
lar, has been described as technique. Leston Havens, for instance, has written a book about Sullivanian technique and describes this as a conscious decision on Sullivan's part to
approach the young man obliquely so not to elicit excess anxiety.[8] In other words, it is a strategy of technique that is appropriate to Sullivan's concept of the schizophrenic dilemma.

But why such a strange, crusty, Edwardian indirection, so
different than his first comment to himself? There are other
ways of being oblique. Essentially Sullivan is making an interpretation of content. He is saying to the patient something of
what he thinks the parents have done. But he is also makig
another interactional communication. He is saying to the patient: I am aware that you are aware that what you are saying
about your parents' beneficence is sheer boloney. You do not
believe it but you expect me to believe it because you think
we are all hypocrites aligned against you. I'm not stupid enough
to try to be friendly toward you because you would think I'm
trying to butter you up, but I thought I would let you know
that I'm in on the game. Now, that sounds rather more like
R.D. Laing and of course it may not be what Sullivan had in
mind at all. But it seems to me it is equally as probable as the
idea that he was simply trying to spare the patient anxiety by
a studied indirection. In essence it is a very complex communication to the patient about the layering-upon-layer of awareness in his life, in Laingian paradox, about what he doesn't
know he knows about what he doesn't know he knows.

What then if the patient withholds information from the
therapist? This seems at first glance a bizarre way of doing therapy. The "basic rule" of psychoanalysis is that the patient say

what comes to mind. If he won't, we say we don't have a "working alliance." Yet, almost all patients withhold; events are "forgotten," and remembered only after a focusing interpretation of the analyst. We rather take these lapses for granted, appreciate that the patient is anxious; but we rarely consider that withholding is a perfectly normative social skill and that the patient is exercising it. Perfect patients don't seem to do much better in therapy than perfect children do in life.

When a therapist enforces the "basic rule," he usually gets a flurry of thinking the unthinkable: the patient, especially if on the couch, comes up with every unacceptable hostile and sexual fantasy he can contrive. Most analysts sensibly dismiss this material. In this case, the patient feels he must give up his symptom to the analyst who, in essence, tells him to keep it. After all, he is only distressed about the revelation of it to others. What family therapists would call a "paradoxical injunction" works. The therapist "joins" the symptom. The patient doesn't lose it; he loses interest in it. Why should this work? Possibly because the therapist is focusing not on the meaning of a symptom to the patient but on the meaning of the symptom as it exists in interaction with the therapist.

This defines a very important distinction in the direction of therapeutic movement. From the intrapsychic perspective, behavior with the therapist is carried over, transferred, from the outside world. As Menninger and Philip Holzman put it:

. . . the patient successively goes from the contemporary situation to the analytic situation, thence to related aspects of the childhood situation, thence to the reality situation and on around the circle in the same *counter-clockwise direction* [emphasis added]. This is the typical, proper, and correct sequence. . . . But if successive material tends to move from the depths directly to the present movement, i.e., in what on our diagram is a clockwise direction, something is wrong.[9]

In other words, the direction of flow determines the definition of reality. The patient creates a distortion in the transference, goes from there to his history, sees the connection, and then can *discard* the transferential distortion as unreal. In contrast, if one treats each event with the therapist as a *de novo* and legitimate exchange, then it becomes simply a place to examine in exquisite detail how the patient deals with experience. It is no more or less real than his historical experience and not very different, not because the patient is projecting, but because in his discourse with his world he shapes and perpetuates it. It is through symbols that one not merely knows but constitutes the world. The patient may proceed from past to present or reverse the flow. For the interpersonalist the direction is circular or helical, not linear and unidirectional. To use a simple example: traditionally the patient sees the therapist as a critical father, then goes back to his childhood experience, which he perceived as similarly critical. He then sees that as a distortion in the service of his inner machinery, or, if true, a stimulus to his internal machinery. He returns to the present, aware that his touchiness about his present life and the transference is a distortion carried over from the past.

In contrast, if one concedes that the patient's perception of the therapist as critical has some grain of truth, then one might wonder how he perceives and deals with criticism—both in the here-and-now and in the past. There is no issue of distortion or of helping the patient distinguish what part of his upset is appropriate and what part not. It will develop that he has great difficulty with that aspect of interpersonal behavior dealing with judgment, criticism, helpfulness, advice giving, the entire set of interactions dealing with one person impinging knowledgeably upon the behavior of another; and, most importantly, that this difficulty lies in his inability to delineate and order his experience in language. Sullivan's concept of the therapist as "consensual validator," then, can be taken as the therapist helping the patient distinguish between what is real and what is not (which Sullivan certainly did) or as participating with the patient and, simultaneously, examining with him their nuances of interaction.

Regardless of the therapist's ostensible intent, he cannot help but react to the patient. If the patient is a homosexual, the therapist has his own experience of that. He can try to minimize revealing this to the patient in an effort to keep his participation neutral. One might debate the feasibility and even honesty of that effort. If the patient thinks the therapist is critical, and the therapist is aware of his criticality, then they can explore together what happens when they collide. Being not-critical of something infantile and exploitative can be as much a collusive participation with a patient as being critical out of competition or resentment. An arena of almost infinite nuance opens up. The patient's past, the patient's present, and his interaction with the therapist become *transforms* of each other, immensely useful as different parameters of the same experience.

CHAPTER 6

Praxis: The Common Ground of Therapy

Psychoanalysis extends language beyond
the logical plane of rational discourse to
the alogical regions of life, and in doing
so it makes that part of us speak which is
not so much dumb as it has been
constrained to silence.
—PAUL RICOEUR

EVEN A CLINICIAN who abjures the direction the "nose"
vignette took will recognize something hauntingly familiar
about it. There are the traditional constraints of the
fifty-minute session, fee, the limitation of contact with the
patient to sessions. The patient presents his symptom—an
obsessional preoccupation not with his appearance but with
deception, and withholding. He then, apparently without
awareness of connection, mentions first a change of appointment, which on inquiry turns out to be for a minor surgical
procedure on the much overinvested nose. In the process of
inquiring into why he didn't think to mention it, a childhood
incident in which he withheld information from his parents
reemerges. The therapist then reexamines and revises his own

sense of understanding of the transaction and shifts the focus of his inquiry.

The therapy has proceeded in a circular way, from symptom, to acting-out, to childhood memory, to transference, to countertransference. As I said in the previous chapter, this circling through the material is described by Menninger and is familiar to any psychoanalyst, regardless of theoretical or institutional persuasion. In a word, there is a similarity of method that underlies the difference in purpose. This praxis of psychoanalysis could be defined as Freud's core contribution; it is an act that can be held separate from metapsychology. It is possible to break the psychoanalytic praxis into a series of systematic steps that can be followed methodically. Such a procedure is called an algorithm. As I stated earlier, the success of an algorithm does not depend on the correctness of its theoretical underpinnings. It is possible to have an algorithm that works although the theoretical explanation of its efficacy is incorrect or incomplete.

Much empirical wisdom works that way. In the Middle Ages it was known that night air caused the ague. Consequently, windows were sealed, plants removed from rooms, and beds heavily muffled in hangings. It was also known that the night vapors were worse in low lands, so whenever possible people built their houses on high land. They did not, of course, know about the anopheles mosquito carrying the parasite of malaria. They used the paradigm of Aristotle's humors and devised an algorithm for preventing the ague. The paradigm may be wrong or, to our eyes, naïve; and yet, the algorithm may work. Freud's paradigm was Newtonian and energic. But his algorithm is pragmatic and not paradigm-bound. To put it more simply, the theory can be separated from the therapy and may not even have very much connection.

The algorithm can be divided into three steps:

Praxis: The Common Ground of Therapy

1. The establishment and definition of the therapeutic frame.
2. The elaboration and enrichment of implicate and explicate order in the patient's life.
3. The elucidation of this order in the therapist-patient relationship.

I shall elaborate these three highly condensed steps, but I would emphasize again that this algorithm is at the core of any psychoanalytic position, from the most conservative to the most radical interpersonal. A rational, detailed inquiry, in which scotomata and inconsistencies are pointed out to the patient and in which the therapist attempts to interpret "distortion"—that is, to point out to the patient where he is distorting reality—falls short of psychoanalysis by anyone's stringent definition. Nor is a therapy that provides the patient an opportunity to get in touch with feelings or to have a healing encounter with a loving and concerned preceptor properly considered psychoanalysis. This is not to deny that these can constitute a rationale for effective psychotherapy, more appropriate for some patients than psychoanalysis. But they do not meet the requirements of the psychoanalytic algorithm.

This is, of course, an extremely arbitrary position, but it approximates Freud's definition of psychoanalysis as any therapy that accepts transference and resistance. As Frederick Crewes put it, "Freud wrote (in 'On Narcissism') that 'the whole structure' of psychoanalysis stands apart from metapsychological propositions, which 'can be replaced and discarded without damaging' that structure. Freud knew that high-level theory was an afterthought to the relatively direct inferences of the consulting room."[1] These terms, "transference" and "resistance," are used more rhetorically than rigorously. Psychoanalysts seem to make a word mean whatever they wish; it is only a question, as Humpty-Dumpty put it, of who is to be master. Still, it is a definition of psychoanalytic praxis that few analysts would disagree with. How they interpret it and how the outcomes differ is another matter altogether.

The "frame" is a concept first introduced by Bateson and since used extensively in sociology and psychoanalysis.[2] It is the conceptual delineation of the constraints of patient-therapist interaction. The physical constraints are the obvious ones: limited contact, time, money, frequency, promptness, cancellations, vacations, and so forth. There is the mutual contract, to endure and to examine what happens between them. The patient is held to the contract of honest effort, reporting of dreams, associations, and commitment to coming even when he doesn't want to.

Simultaneously, a much subtler definition of limits takes place; a structuring by the therapist, within the first few sessions, of the patient's motivations for being in therapy, his goals, his expectations of the therapist. Moreover, in the process of inquiring, the therapist defines and frames *his* own limitations and areas of competence. A patient who has just separated from his wife and is depressed is not necessarily a candidate for psychotherapy of any sort or, less so, for psychoanalytic therapy. A therapy in which the patient wanders in, states his complaints vaguely, and extracts a tacit agreement from the therapist to treat him has already violated the rigorous constraints of the algorithm. The patient frequently comes into therapy to perfect his neurosis. It is the function of the therapist to create a field of omission, to warn the patient that he will fail him, in that respect. The frame constrains the therapist as well as the patient.

To repeat, the first step is essentially a definition of limits. That means not simply the physical framing of the therapy but defining the limits of possibilities, the limits of commitment, the limits of interest. This may include such embarrassingly mundane issues as how busy the therapist is, who referred the patient, the relative ages of therapist and patient, issues of comparative socioeconomic status. There may be vaguer aesthetic issues: is the patient attractive to the therapist; does he/she remind him/her of someone from his past; is he interested in what the patient does or how he lives? The therapist is *never* without motive. He does not begin the therapy cleansed of purpose, and the patient who must believe in this Parsifal-like purity is already entangled in a paranoid net. The therapist must actualize his variables, not exclude them—the latter, a patent impossibility. In countertransference, as was said of the Minié ball, in the Civil War, "You never hear the one that gets you." What is known of the therapist's participation is grist for the mill; what is out of his awareness is what causes problems. Conscious or preconscious awareness of a therapist's motives can be used effectively as a therapeutic instrument, even when it is indisputably "countertransferential."

Khan has a marvelous vignette in his treatment of a very attractive young demimondaine who had been exposed to an elegant seduction by her uncle.[3] Dr. Khan arranged to see her on Sunday, charged her a reduced fee, saw her irregularly, on demand. He, of course, did not define this as a psychoanalytic therapy but as an attenuated "psychotherapy."

After violating the traditional constraints of the frame, making special arrangements for her, for no apparent reason other than her attractiveness, Dr. Khan then proceeded to treat her with circumspection and genuine solicitude. She would appear for sessions (on the couch) in miniskirts and see-through blouses and make seductive overtures. Dr. Khan conceives an extremely elaborate hypothesis about her wish to be a boy, and she responds very well to treatment. Was it because of the accuracy of Dr. Khan's formulations or his paradoxical manipulation of the frame? Although he does not say so, I suspect this was a deliberate strategy. She would not have tolerated a traditional psychoanalytic frame. By his first seducing and then not seducing her, she was given an opportunity to play through and resolve issues of trust and reliability. It is psychoanalytic psychotherapy; the transference and countertransference is utilized and manipulated but never made explicit and analyzed. For treatment to be fully realized as psychoanalysis, the relationship of therapist and patient with all its nuances and ambiguities must be made explicit.

There is also a temporal dimension to framing. Besides what is talked about, the therapist establishes a very deliberate pacing—neither too rushed nor too slow. The therapist avoids—either by silences, grunts, detailed inquiry, or interpretations—being flooded by material or a loss of therapeutic impulsion. The eager neophyte, wrestling enthusiastically with the material, may find a year later that he is bogged down with a passive, dulled patient. In a successful treatment, the patient carries the therapy. As I shall describe in the next chapter, the sine qua non of therapy, the capacity of the therapist to make connections, to hear the "line" of associations depends on the paced impulsion of the patient's process. Hermeneutics notwithstanding, this sense of timing and pace may be the single most important factor in establishing a working milieu.

To add a somewhat irreverent proxemic simile, it is a bit like lion taming. The tamer must locate precisely his training distance; if he gets too close, the lion charges him; too far, and the beast loses interest. So it is with patients; one finds the working distance and slowly retreats. Hopefully, the patient comes forth. Perhaps a more dignified comparison would be to Martin Buber's concept of dialogue that depends on both *relation* and *distance*. One both enters the interhuman relationship and simultaneously puts the other at a distance. This is a point Buber made specifically for a psychoanalytic audience in 1957.[4]

There exists a very wide range of framing from the loose boundaries of, say, Sándor Ferenczi to the virtual stockade established by Charles Brenner or Robert Langs. "Framing" lends itself metaphorically to the idea that one is simply putting an arbitrary boundary around a piece of life, just as the frame of a landscape defines the piece of real estate the artist has chosen to portray. Thus, one might think of the psychoanalytic setting as focusing the patient's life or creating a microcosm of life for the patient to experience, for first-hand corrective experience with reality.

This misses the essential nature of the psychoanalytic setting and misconstrues the purpose of the constraints. As Bateson pointed out, psychoanalysis is a game: it is structured *play;* it is not real life. Freud, too, referred to the transference as a "playground." Still, this is a point likely to offend anyone who equates play with not being serious or with triviality. No such pejoration is intended. Play is serious business; games can be played to the death. The psychoanalytic frame does not simply focus one's eye; it establishes a set of rules. As Bateson put it, "The first step in defining a psychological frame might be to say that it is (or delimits) a class or set of messages (or meaningful actions)."[5]

Play, by definition, is not what it purports to be. As Bateson pointed out, a nip is not a bite; that is, the dog playing pretends to bite but does not really threaten his playmate. The dog's metamessage is in his rear end: the front of the dog growls, lays back its ears, bares its teeth; the rear end is elevated, the tail wags. The metamessage is, "This is play!" Puppies are sometimes killed by adult dogs when they misread the message. Psychoanalysis is feasible as a treatment modality only because it is play. Otherwise, the patient would simply be having an experience with another person, certainly an expert, a well-intentioned one, but, judging from analysts' personal lives, no better or worse than the rest of mankind. The analyst is freed by the metamessage of the frame, "This is play," to experience himself in a different fashion—if nothing else, to be less anxious—since it is one thing if one's patient never hears anything one says, quite another thing if it is one's mate.

The frame, then, is not a contract in real life, but a highly delimited piece of play, with hierarchical sets of metamessages, and *it is this very layering of message and meaning that psychoanalysts explore.* This becomes readily evident when one encounters a patient who cannot make the distinction. The patient does not develop a "positive transference"; he falls madly in love (or hate) with the therapist and expects it to be reciprocated. We call this kind of early erotic transference "ominous" and the patient "concretized," with unstable boundaries. Really, the patient doesn't know how or refuses to play the game. A simpler example is the patient who slyly asks, "If you really care about me, why don't you treat me for nothing?" The therapist either maintains silence or lamely explains that, without the fee, the patient would not be really "committed to change." The truth is that we are not the patient's friend but his analyst. It is not a lesser category or a less concerned one: it is simply different. Again, to quote Bateson:

> The resemblance between the process of therapy and the phenomenon of play is, in fact, profound. Both occur within a delimited psychological frame, a spatial and temporal bounding of a set of interactive messages. In both play and therapy, the messages have a special and peculiar relationship to a more concrete and basic reality. Just as the pseudocombat of play is not real combat, so also the pseudolove and pseudohate of therapy are not real love and hate.[6]

From the Freudian viewpoint, this defines the playground in which regression can take place and the patient can experience his fantasy distortions. From the interpersonal perspective, it is a situation of augmented and clarified semiotic message rendered unique by the framing and permitting patient and therapist an opportunity to examine the layering of semiotic experience first-hand.

CHAPTER 7

Praxis: The Field of Play

Whatever the tense used, all utterance is
a present act. Remembrance is always
now.

—GEORGE STEINER

HAVING ESTABLISHED the frame, the therapist can proceed to playing the game, either by encouraging free association, or by a Sullivanian, detailed inquiry that more formally
pursues the lacunae, the omissions in the patient's story. In either case, the therapist expands and enriches *data*. This material emerges along a number of parameters: obviously, the patient's present life and its difficulties, which have brought him
into therapy; his past history and family experience, which pre-
destined his present difficulties; his dreams and fantasies,
which represent leaks in his organized perceptions of his life.
Material also emerges from his experience with the therapist
and the therapist's experience with him, but that will be taken
up at a later point.

An extraordinary order begins to emerge. It can be noted
that the same patterning of experience is evident whether one
takes one small incident and explores it in great "depth," or
if one takes a panoramic overview of the patient's data. One
can (and persuasive instructors often do) take the first ten min-

utes of a session and reconstruct virtually the patient's entire dynamics. Moreover, if one proceeds methodically from present to history to transference (or, according to Menninger, from present to transference to history), one sees the same patterning repeated in each area. A helical movement (a three-dimensional, expanding spiral) is established, since on each circling of the different parameters of data, the patterning appears more extensive within each parameter and in the overview. There is an extraordinary *implicate order.*

In other words, the play begins with enrichment of data, expands to matching data from different parameters of experience, including imaginary (fantasy) ones, and culminates with the therapist and patient detecting an enlarged and enriched pattern that the therapist "interprets" (that is, formulates), which is, in itself, a participation in the patterning that "kicks" the circular movement around again, on a "higher" and wider spiral.

It is this emphasis on the carry-over of pattern and meaning from one parameter to another that underlay Freud's correlation of obsessionality, miserliness, anality. The patient's "anal-retentiveness" could be seen extending across the entire range of his experience Freud would have said the patient was fixated at the anal level; one might, with equal accuracy, say that withholding is the *metaphor* used by the patient. The analyst's focus on metaphoric transformations led Lionel Trilling to call psychoanalysis the "science of Tropes"; that is, literary metaphor.[1]

The following is a very simple clinical example. A patient has three dreams together. In one dream, he is dealing with his Chinese laundry man, who is giving him trouble about getting his shirt back. In the second dream, he is in a restaurant, and although he has a reservation he is being made to wait for his table. In the third dream, he is in a bank trying to obtain a loan, and he is being asked to pay some outrageous interest. The theme running through all three is frustration at dealing with some functionary who is giving him a hard time. The dreams express his difficulty with authority figures and his complex attitudes about frustration, disappointment, and disapproval. But every analyst immediately hears something else in these dreams. He hears them as transferential dreams. Why? Because inscrutability and rigid, unforgiving time and money arrangements are all three strongly characteristic of the psychoanalytic setting.

The therapist can formulate this inherent patterning in a variety of ways ranging from the most operational to the most obtruse hermeneutical. The interpretive set is the therapist's metaphor; it is merely a way of commenting on what he is observing—if you will, a digital, linear observation of a complex, multilayered, analogic process. But the patterning *emerges from the patient,* takes form quite without conscious effort, as he talks. As Khan said, "We are the servants of the patient's process."[2]

Without going far afield at this point into neuropsychological speculations, it seems reasonable to assume that this remarkable phenomenon reflects some intrinsic brain organization. This is a point well worth emphasizing, since therapists sometimes act as if the therapy depended on their ability to make sense out of a chaotic flow; to bring order out of chaos, a godly and unwarranted presumption. The order is there for the therapist *and* the patient to hear. If they do not hear it today, they will tomorrow as the data multiply and the complexity increases.

So, having established the constraints of the frame, we observe a process that does not take place in real life but is an artifact of the therapy. As the patient ranges across parameters of experience, paced and supported and catalyzed by the therapist, a pervasive coherence emerges. The therapist, by matching patterns, can delineate a larger metapattern that in turn throws light on the individual areas of inquiry, which again enriches and enlarges the patterning.

For example, another patient, a woman in her late forties, has had a long series of psychoanalytic treatments, with a variety of perspectives represented. She is at a major crisis point in her life, concerning work and marital relationship. A crucial paradigmatic memory in therapy, an iconic memory (not arrived at in the therapy), is of a period in her childhood from age eleven to thirteen when, every Sunday, her mother would leave the house with her youngest sister and she would remain with her father. He was an opera buff and would insist that she lie down on the bed with him and listen to the radio opera. She would acquiesce; according to her reports, would lie rigidly next to him without any snuggling or holding until he would doze off, usually in an hour or so. At that point, she would slip away with a feeling of great relief. Neither he nor she would mention her having left. She apparently never told him in so many words that she hated to be there and that she felt constrained, tied down, which is her present representation of the event.

Years of therapy have made her cognizant of the likely formulations: to wit, she wanted to be there, that there was an unconscious sexual collusion, or that the long period of this involvement is a fantasy; perhaps it happened only once or twice. Or, that she is misrepresenting or misremembering her participation, that it was not rigid or perhaps that the entire incident was warm and enjoyable. The hermeneutic approach is to try to arrive at the fantasy distortions of the patient. She must be wrong about some part of it. Note that nothing has really changed in her perception of the event after years of therapeutic effort.

Suppose we agree that it occurred as she presented it. Then we might ask, why didn't she object, say no, leave the house, go with her mother? Why didn't her father notice that she was stiff and unhappy? Note that whether we look for her unconscious collusive fantasy or wonder why she didn't take action and clear out, we are saying to her, in essence, "It's your fault that this went on; you could have stopped it." To either approach, she responds with stiff acquiescence and the therapist is defeated.

Suppose on the other hand, that when she tells the story one thinks, "So what? What does she want from me? Why am I interested in revising her perception of the story? I've moved from the historical inquiry to a transaction with her *around* the material, that transaction being a transformation of the material, because she wouldn't have told me, to begin with, *except* as a transaction; that is, she is saying, "I am telling you this so you will react to it and participate with me around it." It must be so, since this is the nature of language. She is talking *to me* (qua therapist) about something that happened to her. The question then becomes not what really happened to her or what her symbolic distortion of the real event is, but what is she doing with me now and how am I participating?

The obvious implication is that we shall recapitulate the relationship with her father. She will lie stiffly next to me, never indicate her resistance but never relent, and she will sneak away at the first opportunity. My experience is that I pursue this issue with great good will, patience, and commitment. Why? Why, like the father, doesn't the therapist hear that she is in a rage, by her own description, and doesn't want to be here? The question then becomes to examine this bind we have in reality recapitulated. She is, by the way, never warm or affectionate or interested. At the same time, she somehow manages to keep one's interest, seeming appealing, attractive, and likable. This is somehow a kind of acting skill. (She was an actress.) The message then is semiotically layered: she resists stiffly, doesn't want to be here, constrained by me, but I'm not to notice, still be interested in her, assume that she is interested in being with me without any confirmation from her. This requires a series of metamessages.

If I am to avoid intrapsychic mechanisms of explanation, how to explain this "repetition compulsion?" The therapist does not hermeneutically identify the ostensibly correct message; for example, "You want to have an erotic but denied relationship with your father." Rather, he is involved in a participatory exegesis, an expansion of the complexity. A theory of unconscious motives, of course, implies intentionality. It may not be so. The mind may be an automatic self-equilibrating mechanism. The point is that the patient is not distorting the relationship with me; it *is* a replication of the situation with her father and requires my participation. The paradox is that if I don't take part, she might not stay; if I do participate, she will not change. Semiotic ambiguity leads to anxiety. Why? One could say she doesn't want to come into touch with powerful feelings about her father: love, hate, erotic feelings. But real affect is disequilibrating in this situation. To feel strongly is to lose one's balance, and the ambiguities require a sustained alertness. I would claim that she may not be afraid of strong feelings per se but the *consequences* of strong feeling.

To repeat: the stream of consciousness comes from the patient. The therapist and patient collaborate to put it into language. This constitutes an effective core of psychotherapy, but it is not yet psychoanalysis. Associative expansion or detailed inquiry with formulations and pattern delineation is not psychoanalysis until the effect of the formulation, the participation of the therapist, is taken into account. In psychoanalysis, the therapist becomes part of what he sets out to cure, and it is the assessment of his contribution and the form of his amalgamation into the patient's system that give psychoanalysis its particular power. A frame and an inquiry with interpretation is psychotherapy: *psychoanalysis is distinguished by the infinite regress of its data within a fixed frame.* The game players are in a metagame in which they observe the first game. A third game observes the second, and so on. Infinite regress is at the core of both the Freudian concept of transference and Sullivanian participant-observation.

All language-oriented psychotherapies recognize that the relationship with the therapist resonates to, or recapitulates, other dimensions of the patient's life. If that relationship is utilized deliberately to lever the patient into changing, then the therapist is engaged in an instructive process. It may be effective as corrective emotional experience or benign authoritative psychotherapy, but it is not psychoanalysis. In psychoanalysis, the patient-therapist relationship is used to facilitate a further expansion of data. For the intrapsychic therapist the expansion, or regression, is vertical, back in time, deeper. For the interpersonalist, the regression is horizontal, mapping wider patterns of interaction. This is not to say that the traditionalists are not interested in the present or that the interpersonalists are not interested in the past; but for the former, the past is impacted on the present. For the latter, the past and present lie on an experiential continuum.

Let us consider, as an example, a male patient's talking about his anger at his father. He begins to *feel* rage as he talks. Very good. Let us suppose that he realizes he has been guilty about being angry at his father. A noxious fantasy has been dispelled. But a sneaking thought enters. After all, he treats his own children much as his father treated him. Maybe his father was correct: *he* is impossible, unlovable. Or, maybe he wouldn't take any criticism from the father, even if it were justified.

Another shift occurs. Perhaps the therapist is patronizingly *encouraging* his anger, because it is "good for him." Or, maybe, the therapist is diverting anger from himself. There was a brief exchange earlier in the session, in which the patient complained about the therapist's lateness, his having stopped the previous session earlier, his seeming bored. Now the therapist has become the father. There are real aspects of the therapist's behavior that fit the image of the father. Father, too, never got angry openly, simply withdrew. Is the patient projecting on to the therapist from his past? Has the therapist in "projective identification" become the father? Now the patient gets angry at the therapist, who doesn't seem to mind very much. He learns his anger will not kill the therapist. Or does he? Perhaps the therapist is upset and not showing it openly. An observer might have noticed that the therapist is clutching the arms of his chair. Perhaps the therapist is too damned arrogant to care about the patient's anger—it's all make-believe, anyhow.

It is only when the patient is frightened by his anger at the therapist and the therapist uncomfortable by the anger of the patient that an authentic exchange begins. Here the patient is not frightened at his anger but at the interpersonal ramifications set into motion by his anger. The metamessages are becoming obscure. The therapist could be lying or unaware of his feelings, if he denies being upset. The patient no longer trusts the game, which is what the game is all about. It is out of this fearful confusion that the patient begins to grasp how complex and inattended much of what has been going on in his life is.

He may then try another shift of perspective, try on another version "for size": perhaps my father was not really a bad guy after all. Maybe I sided against him with my mother because I was her favorite. He will expand that view of the data and then shift that posture into the relationship with the therapist and again try it out.

Will he arrive at the right answer? I doubt if there is one. I suspect that cure emerges from the successive enrichments of perspective as this circling through the data proceeds. The dream of the optimal insight, the "Aha! at last I see that . . . " is an ever-elusive Holy Grail. I don't believe it happens, because life is not that simple. If it were, one would be having bad experiences but not, from my viewpoint, the mystification that makes for neurosis. Unmystified parental abuse makes for angry people, perhaps psychopathic ones, but not for neurosis. The neurotic crimes are either crimes of omission, the failure to provide an experience that cannot be clearly missed because it was never experienced; or crimes of commission that are so obscured that the patient cannot define them.

Children, I have noted, will tolerate and even show compassion for severe parental defects, as long as they are clear what it is that is wrong and clear that it is not their doing.

The significant insights in therapy, and they do occur, are not solutions but *connections*—connections drawn between previously unrelated events. Much of the excitement of the therapeutic play is the sense of seeing first-hand how things hang together. What, after all, was the Sphinx's riddle?—an analogy requiring a novel shift of perspective, seeing a connection that was heretofore unapparent: four legs, two legs, three—*Man!*

CHAPTER 8

Praxis: Uses of the Transference

Words are also deeds.
—Ludwig Wittgenstein

THE THIRD and most definitive step of the psychoanalytic algorithm is the utilization of the patient-therapist transaction: classically, as a screen on which the patient can project his fantasies; as the object-relationship therapist would have it, as a mirror in which he can see his self (not himself) reflected; or, from an interpersonal reference, as an interactional field that can be observed as it takes place. From the intrapsychic viewpoint, the therapist's participation is unwanted, a warp in the screen, a flaw in the mirror. From the interpersonal view, it is intrinsic to the dialogic participation which is the *vis a tergo* of therapy.

All psychoanalysts would agree that the patterning of the patient-therapist field is redundant; that is, that it repeats the patterning noted in other parameters of the therapy. It is at this point that the parting of the roads occurs and the implications are immense. An entirely different paradigm is implicit;

from giving the patient an arena in which to actualize and contact his fantasies, we have gone to participating with him in what may be called a *language-act*. The focus has become language.

It must be understood that when the therapist talks with the patient, he *behaves* with him. Therefore, every verbal exchange (and those are the only ones officially sanctioned), every interpretation, consists of a piece of behavior with the patient and then a commentary, in speech, on that behavior. The commentary, the content of the interpretation, is, then, our old friend, the metamessage. From this perspective, the classical effort to purge interpretations of all participatory intent seems illusory. The therapist cannot help but be there.

When psychoanalysts of different persuasions settle down to examine clinical data, it is in a virtual field of straw men replete with murmurs of "Of course, we take that into account . . ." It is therefore necessary to examine what therapists commit to print, since we may assume that the written word represents their considered position and bears the imprimatur of their editors. It is unfortunately true that any clinical presentation, particularly a written one, is so adumbrated as to have the vitality of a pinned butterfly. Any effort to "present" clinical material is simultaneously an act of courage and a murder. Even unkinder things may be said of attempting an exegesis of someone else's presentation. But the consequences of underestimating one's interaction with the patient are crucial and must be examined.

I wish to use a brief part of a case presentation by Charles Feigelson as an example of a therapist's attempt to treat his participation as neutral.[1] Dr. Feigelson, a faculty member of the New York Psychoanalytic Institute, defines the psychoanalytic technique in this way: "We interpret defenses, we interpret what is defended against, we interpret the reasons for the defense."[2] He also quotes Freud's caveat on focused attention that would lead to the therapist's selection, unwittingly, of the data. Thus, neutrality is enforced, if the therapist maintains "evenly suspended attention."[3]

Feigelson tells of a thirty-four-year-old homosexual man. It is important, first, to note that there is no question, in the mind of either the therapist or the patient, that a successful outcome of the treatment will make him heterosexual. Moreover, it is clear that the patient agrees that he has come into therapy in order to relinquish his homosexuality. The patient has apparently, with some persuasion from the therapist, just had his first heterosexual experience with a prostitute. He did not particularly enjoy the experience and felt removed, but not repulsed.

He reports the following dream: "I was in a Spanish-style house; there was a room which had cracked walls, like the canvas had been torn away. It was like a room that I had canvassed for my mother; it was wet and moist." As he described the wet, moist sensations, he began to experience them, and this suddenly reminded him of the sexual feelings with the woman, and he was somewhat surprised that he had previously dissociated this awareness of the feeling of intercourse. In the dream, in the room, there were feces coming out of the cracked walls. Walking around in this Spanish house was the Pope; he was a benevolent Pope, and he felt in his dream that he was being somewhat irreverent. There was also a tiny bull lodged in some concrete or cement, and it had shiny gold horns." The patient talked about the horns as representing penises, and he thought how much damage they could do.

Feigelson's interpretation is that the patient had felt the sexual experience was like being in a bullfight and that "his precious golden horns would be dirtied by the woman's crack." The patient responded to this by wondering who would be the bull and who would be the matador. He felt that the woman would be the matador and that he would be killed. "It was the experience of wet and moist that came to him as part of his dream experience that helped him to know that his dream had to do with his sexual experience. It lent conviction to the interpretation of the dream."

To begin with, the interpretation made by the analyst utilizes only a small part of the imagery in the dream—that part of the manifest content which supports the therapist's formulation of the significant theme, the "latent content." Any interpretation is not only a perception of meaning in the dream, but it is a participation, a piece of behavior on the therapist's part. The therapist tells him that his sexual experience was "like a bullfight" and that his "precious golden horns would be dirtied by the woman's dirty crack." The use of words like "precious" and "dirty crack" and the attitude of the interpretation imply that the therapist is indicating some scorn and disapproval of the patient's fastidiousness and repulsion by female genitalia. The therapist is taking a rather forceful, macho position, as if to model for the patient an appropriate role. So, one has both the content of the interpretation (which, albeit possibly correct, is limited) and second, the behavior and metacommunication of the therapist *around* the content, which pressures the patient toward a heterosexual adjustment.

In the dream, the room has cracked walls "like the canvas had been torn away. It was like a room that I had canvassed for my mother." The cracks in the wall, the peeling "canvas," and the references to feces coming through the wall could also certainly imply something about his experience in a real sense with his mother. One might suspect that she was either psychotic or in some way very unreliable as a mother figure. This is not in any sense taken up later in the material. Why was it a Spanish-style house? There is one suggestion from the material that the patient is of Latin origin, either Spanish or Italian, although that is never made explicit. Now, why the Pope? No comment is made on the obvious verbal pun of the papal "bull." A papal bull is, of course, an official document, edict, or decree from the Pope. One way of conceptualization is in Jacques Lacan's or Martin Heidegger's sense of the hidden archaeology of words. It is also metonymy; that is, a partial concept that stands for a larger whole. The literal meaning of "bull" is from the Latin *bulla,* meaning a knob or seal, originally a seal affixed to a document, especially to one from the Pope. It would seem that the transference implication of the dream was that the Pope ("Papa" in Italian, or father or analyst) was attaching his paternal seal to the patient's heterosexuality or to something in his relationship with women or his mother. Moreover, it is a tiny bull, it is embedded in cement, and it has shiny golden horns. The contrast between the gold of the horns and the rest of the bull implies something about the patient's ambiguous feelings about the value of the papal injunction. One might suspect from this, in a transferential mode, that he has some marked misgivings or ambiguity about the value of the therapist's help, particularly in pressuring him to be heterosexual.

If one were to postulate that instead of an oedipal castration anxiety, as the therapist formulates it, there is a much deeper terror and distrust of the mothering person, one might have been inclined to pursue more what his experience had been with his mother. However, the patient does become heterosexual in the course of therapy (certainly no small effect), but one might wonder whether it was the validity of the interpretation that brings about his heterosexuality or the model of the therapist as a powerful, somewhat disdainful father who pushes him through his phobic terror of women. Paradoxically, he may very well have become heterosexual as a submission to his therapist. Perhaps his problem is resolved; or perhaps his terror of the woman is simply pushed much deeper underground. One can become heterosexual as a homosexual submission!

Interestingly enough, in a series of subsequent dreams presented in the clinical material, the issue of the patient's hostility toward the father and fear of the father and fear of killing the father is focused. But hostility is never discussed in relation to the therapist! It is never focused as an issue in the transference clustered around a real issue between the therapist and the patient: the patient's becoming heterosexual because the therapist considers homosexuality "pathological." Supposing the material had gone in another direction—namely, to investigate the patient's feeling that he had to be a good boy and become heterosexual, because that is the way to be, because that is the only way he can win the father's approval and love. This might have released him to be heterosexual; or it might have given him the room to explore what might underlie his homosexuality, some kind of terror and rage towards the woman. This would also open the possibility of exploring what actually went on in his childhood home and to what extent the father colluded in not permitting him to see something about the mother's mothering. Or did the father insist on an obsessional heterosexuality to cover his own homosexual attachment with his son, or *his* horror of women?

The patient would understand not only that he is afraid of his father, afraid of killing his father, and afraid of his father's rage, but also that he is horrified by his mother, frightened of all sorts of dimensions of his experience with mothering, that he perhaps prefers homosexuality and should stay a homosexual, that he has an autonomous decision to make about what really interests him sexually and how he wants to live his life. He might come out of the therapy a satisfied homosexual, or a heterosexual for conventional reasons, or a heterosexual because of a genuine change of erotic object.

Any therapist's "interpretations" do not talk to the patient's unconscious; they are *acts* with the patient that influence his participation in the therapy. In addition, they serve to divert the patient from what the therapist is *doing* with what he is saying. The patient's symptom, his homosexuality, does not disappear, like Rumpelstiltskin, because its name is known, but because of his experience with the therapist. In a more interpersonal mode, the emphasis would be on the observation and reporting of the therapist's participation, as noted by the patient in the dream and as validated by the therapist's awareness of his own investment in the patient's change.

Psychoanalysis is not what Anna O. so felicitously named the "talking cure"; rather, it is the cure that reestablishes the relationship *between* talk and behavior. *Psychoanalysis deals with what is said about what is done.* Leo Stone called speech "the veritable stuff of psychoanalysis." More recently, Paul Ricoeur has said that "there enters into the field of investigation only that part of experience which is capable of being said."[4] I quote these two contemporary sources to affirm that this is by no means a vestigial concept. Yet, we know that all the talk in the world doesn't change patients, that persuasive formulations of psychodynamics can fall flat, and that neophyte analysts more often talk too much than too little. It seems that what these authors really imply is that psychoanalysis is the *nonacting* cure; that is, what is acted out, not talked about, cannot be encompassed in the treatment. This would certainly be consistent with Freud's position in "Remembering, Repeating, and Working Through": "He [the therapist] celebrates it as a triumph for the treatment if he can bring it about that something that the patient wishes to discharge in action is disposed of through the work of remembering."[5]

But the distinction between speech and action is often very obscure. Some acting-out seems clearly more like a vivid nonverbal language than pure evasion; and it is often precisely at this elusive interface of action and speech that the most impressive psychoanalytic insights take place. Consider the patient who announces that he could not possibly be angry at the therapist and then kicks over the latter's cocktail table; or the therapist who is unaware of his anger with a patient and finds, to his horror, that he has forgotten to appear for a session. These examples might be considered simple parapraxes, yet they are one end of a continuum of behavior that ranges through more precise symbolic reenactments of psychoanalytic content onto a far subtler resonance between the subject material—the "talk" of therapy—and the patterning of the transference, the behavior.

For example, a patient dreams she is sitting in a Japanese restaurant, unable to decipher the menu. At a table next to her sits a man with graying hair who holds the menu up in the air and points out to her a rather simple shrimp dish. She now knows what to order. When asked what she makes of this dream (she does not volunteer), the patient replies, "At first, it didn't make any sense to me, but then I thought to myself, what would *you* say about it?" She then proceeds to present a quite sophisticated explication of the transference aspects of the dream, and, indeed, some of the countertransference implications. Does she not *play out* between us the content of the dream? She must read the therapist's instructions (even if they are "simple" or "tiny"). She does it everywhere: she can only arrive at a decision by first applying the template of someone else's experience. Surely, all this between us is mediated through speech; but is it not also action, speech-as-behavior?

The debate begins to sound sadly familiar. Is it acting-out, acting-in, or parapraxis? Should the term "acting-out" be limited only to behavior that repeats earlier infantile experience?

It seems much the same ambiguity that pervades the discussion of countertransference. What is real, what is not real, what is regression, how much "participation" is permissible on the part of the therapist? The distinctions so clear to Otto Fenichel and Menninger become, for many of us, increasingly obscure. If transference is the "playground" Freud considered it to be, what happens in the playground?[6] If there is regression in the transference, is it only talked about? Can it be only talked about because the therapist will not play? Or, is the transference a variety of that old playground activity, Show and Tell? These dilemmas have been increasingly festooned with metapsychological elaborations designed to bridge the widening gap between orthodox restraint and more radical participant observation. We see this particularly in object-relations theory and its application to borderline syndromes, where much emphasis is put on appropriate and useful responses. It is, to some extent, like bolstering a sinking house by adding another story. Certainly we must agree that speech mediates therapy, but why not look at the nature of the medium, in addition to what is carried?

This apparent dilemma about talk and action—about what is capable of being said and what needs to be shown—is, I suspect, more apparent than real, developing out of a series of misconstruings about the nature of language and its role in psychoanalysis. The confusion begins with the failure to distinguish between speech and language. Ferdinand de Saussure, the Swiss linguist, clearly delineates *parole et langue.*[7] Parole is, of course, "talk," the spoken aspect of language. Language is, in de Saussure's aphorism, "speechless speaking." It is the whole set of linguistic habits that allow an individual to understand and be understood. That is, it encompasses those conventions, rules, or givens that govern the syntax, grammar, and semantics of the spoken communication as it emerges from this matrix.*

Further, as I indicated in chapter 5, one must distinguish between language and semiotics, first defined and named by C.S. Peirce. To repeat Anthony Wilden's definition, semiotics refers to "the transmission of signals, signs, signifiers, and symbols in any communication system whatever." In the hierarchical ordering there is speech, then the intricate machinery for processing speech (language), and finally a more extensive system of coded communication, which involves speech, nonverbal cueings, and, most important, the cultural and social context, the "pragmatics" of communication.† Psychoanalysts have traditionally been concerned with pragmatics. Lacan, the stormy petrel of French psychoanalysis, with his emphasis on "symbolic, real, and imaginary" imagery, seems primarily interested in the semantics of semiotics. His preoccupation with the "word" (with meaning) makes him very difficult for psychoanalysts (or anyone else, for that matter) to read, since there is absolutely no pragmatic base for applicability of his position.[9] It's all very well to claim (from the structuralist viewpoint, correctly) that the unconscious is structured like a language. But how does one talk to it?

It must be understood, then, that speech, spoken language, is only a small part of an extensive semiotic communication that occurs between the two participants in the analytic process. I am suggesting something considerably more elaborate

---

*This distinction between speech and language is perhaps most vividly illustrated by ethological studies with chimpanzees, which have no speech capacity but considerably more language resources than we had heretofore suspected. Washoe, the first chimpanzee to be cultivated linguistically, had an extensive repertory of sign language symbols and could recognize hundreds more. Lucy, another chimpanzee, was able to construct compound words: "cry-hurt-food" for a hot radish, "dirty cat" for a cat she didn't like. This is certainly semantic creation.

†This can open a can of worms, since the French treat language as more encompassing than semiotics, and the Americans follow the hierarchy I have indicated. See Walker Percy for a discussion of this issue.[8]

than simply the idea that one must also pay attention to how the patient sits or looks. I am suggesting that there are other coded communications, as informational as speech, that take place in the realm of the intersubjective.

To begin with, language is also a form of behavior. This concept is familiar as Bateson's "metacommunication"; that is, every communication is a message and a message about the message.[10] There is quite a bit of literature in this area, but it is generally agreed that the metamessage acts upon the environment, as a "command" or set of instructions. Thus, language does not only communicate but it acts upon the environment. It is a process of making. To put it simply, when we talk with someone, we also act with him. This action or behavior is, in the semiotic sense, coded like a language. *The language of speech and the language of action will be transforms of each other;* that is, they will be, in musical terms, harmonic variations on the same theme. The resultant behavior of the dyad will emerge out of this semiotic discourse.

This has also been implicit in Sullivan's concept of participant observation.[11] In its original, discrete use it meant, I believe, to behave with the patient in a manner that maximized one's communication and minimized distortion. Later it came to mean using one's participation less as an arbiter of reality and more as a source of interactional data. But, ultimately, both from the operational viewpoint and the semiological, it means that every communication is a participation, which changes the communication, which changes the participation. Every line of inquiry, including silence, is a choice of alternative participations. There is no way to be with another person, regardless of the therapist's restraint, without interacting with him.

To understand the effect of an intervention one must consider both the semantics and the pragmatics. The effect depends on the attribution of meaning, plus the behavior of the dyad around what is being said. This is akin to P.F. Strawson's division of a statement into what you are saying and what you are saying about it.[12] In some cases this division is obvious. A therapist can make a quite accurate interpretation out of anger or a need to distance or seduce a patient. The patient will perceive the meaning of the communication in the behavior. But there are subtler implications.

A young woman dreams of being the princess with the pea under her mattress. The therapist suggests that she may be referring to an excessive touchiness or sensitivity to criticism. The patient feels hurt and begins to cry. This kind of resonance between content and behavior illuminates, I believe, the heart of the therapeutic dilemma. The therapist must deal with the content of his interpretation and the simultaneous transformation of his participation in to the role of sadistic accuser. Surely the tearfulness is both confirmation and resistance, and surely any reasonably competent therapist can handle this impasse. One doesn't need semiotics to know how. But, like the man who fornicated quite expertly without knowing what he was doing, the therapist is willy-nilly practicing a semiotic skill. I must agree with Marshall Edelson's claim that psychoanalysis is a semiotic science and that

> linguistic competence—the internalized knowledge of language that is possessed without conscious awareness of it or even the ability to explicate it—is a significant foundation of the psychoanalyst's clinical skill. . . . Much of the understanding the psychoanalyst attributes to empathy, intuition, or conscious or unconscious extralingual information actually derives from his own internalized linguistic (and semiological) competence, of whose nature and existence he may be altogether unaware.[13]

To recapitulate my four postulates: first, speech and language are not coterminous; second, language is to be subsumed under the larger rubric of semiotics; third, language is simultaneously behavior; and last, behavior is structured like a language, or behavior is simultaneously language. Singly these postulates are not terribly radical, but combined, several conclusions become inescapable. First, there is no real discontinuity between speech and action. Secondly, "acting-in" the transference is not something that occurs intermittently at times of distress. It is a semiotic dimension. It goes on continually, and the relationship between the patient and the therapist is played out, over time, in a patterned, structured way. This *discourse of action* is isomorphic with whatever the patient and therapist are talking about. It is also isomorphic with whatever the patient has told the therapist about his outside life in the present and historically. Every dimension of the therapy—history, contemporary issues in the patient's life (and the therapist's), dreams, memories, acting-out, acting-in, transference, countertransference—all are of a piece. The therapist's ability to range across these transformational variations of the patient's themes is, as Edelson's quote affirms, the therapist's true métier.

From this perspective, countertransference cannot be considered a response only to the patient's real and present self. It must be a response across *all* these dimensions. Nor can it be only feeling about the patient; it must also be behavior toward him. We are interested in countertransference not only because it distorts the truth of what we tell the patient but because it determines the way we behave with him. And, it is the correspondence of that behavior with other "languages" of the therapy that makes the treatment go.

Let us suppose that the patient is reporting on inexplicable childhood beatings at the hands of his father. The therapist listens in silence. The patient accumulates and expands his sense of fury and finally abreacts in an explosion of heretofore

suppressed rage. But it is quite likely that the patient is identified with his father, is perhaps subtly sadistic toward his own
children or the therapist. He cannot hate the father without
hating the father-in-himself. Thus his abreaction leads into another morass, namely, his self-loathing. Suppose that the therapist, instead of listening quietly, asks for more details, attempts
to establish what the father was so angry about and what the
context of the beatings was. Certainly this is a different participation. It may undercut the anger, but it may make the father
more comprehensible and release the patient from his
self-loathing. Let us suppose, as a third alternative, that the
therapist listens to the tearful report and thinks to himself, "I
can understand why someone might want to bash this guy."
This may not demonstrate the proper psychoanalytic
sang-froid, but it does cue the therapist in to some aspect of
the patient's behavior that the father found himself impotent
to deal with rationally.

All these constitute initially different participations with the
patient around the same material. One might argue that all
but the inactivity are bad technique. Presumably the patient
will progress along his own trajectory if the therapist stays out
and waits. But silence *is* a participation. It might qualify as
a universal nostrum if the patient always got around to further
explication. But that may not be so; sometimes resolution requires a participation on the part of the therapist, often at some
risk to his neutrality. Sometimes our best results follow countertransferential acting-out, losing our tempers, making mistakes. We may be left with an uneasy feeling that if things had
proceeded properly, nothing would have resulted. Did Sullivan
have this in mind? He is reputed to have said "God keep me
from a therapy that goes well!" The material may never emerge
if action is not taken; sometimes interaction with the patient
must precede explanation. This is particularly true with pa-

tients we label borderline or schizoid. For these distrustful people, the correspondence of word and deed must be very high.

Therapeutic effectiveness, then, depends on the correspondence of "show" and "tell." In the examples I used earlier I focused on the patient's replaying in the dyad the material that is being talked about. What does the *therapist* do? Interpretation is not enough, since an interpretation, factually accurate, can be contextually wrong. A variety of working-through takes place—not analysis of the patient's resistance to the interpretation but, rather, a changing participation with the patient around the material. The therapist must operate with the patient in some way as to be "heard."

Let us take that classical purveyor of therapists' despair, the masochistic patient. What is a sadist? Someone who is kind to a masochist, goes the old joke. Sado-masochistic impasses are not resolved by recourse to interpretations, which progressively become acts of desperation or rage on the part of the therapist. Something must happen between them. The therapist who feels benign is not only remote, he is being sadistic. The therapist who feels kindly is repressing his own rage and is afraid of his sadism. What is left? There is a zen koan: "What do you do when you are hanging over a cliff, holding on with one hand?" "Open your fist" is the answer. The therapist must recognize that there is no way to "hear" the patient without feeling angry and sadistic. There is no way to get that feeling out of the therapy except by dissembling, and a lie in behavior is no less abusive than a lie in speech, so the therapist is, again, sadistic. Perhaps a true discourse requires that the therapist be permitted to feel angry and perhaps even sadistic, but without mystifying or double-binding the patient. This would establish a harmonic integrity between the transference and the rest of the patient's life. The message might be heard and the discourse enriched. I don't know if this is really inevitable, but it seems to me a logical extension and well worth considering. Corrective emotional experiences largely disappear in the tar pit of the patient's self-equilibrating system. I doubt that the patient grows because he is supplied with a nurturing environment. I suspect the patient must be engaged, encountered. If behavior is a language, then it must be heard and reacted to. To be detached from an angry person may be to hear him on the speech level but not to hear him on the level of action.

This is not to imply that all the patient's communications are characterologically fly traps. One can also hear simple requests, quiet messages. To those, the therapist can answer directly. For example, the therapist informs the patient that he is going on vacation. The patient asks, "Oh. Where?" Whether the therapist says nothing, asks for fantasies, or casually or perhaps even enthusiastically tells the patient depends on his "third ear," his unconscious linguistic skills. He could be wrong, but at least he listened. Doctrinaire positions about how one should handle this kind of exchange (for example, the patient *always* feels deserted) seem to me shouting in the wind. Perhaps one should shut up and listen and respond.

There is another genre of exchange that can be found touted as proper technique in a number of books and articles. This example is from Ralph Greenson: a patient points out that when he expresses opinions that match the therapist's, he gets marginal cues of approval; when he doesn't, he is subjected to masked hostile analysis. He documents this position with examples. The therapist, decently and honestly, is amazed at his blind spot. He validates the patient's perception, admits his fault, and then asks, Why do you feel obliged to satisfy my political views?—just at the time when the patient has struck back.[14] He plays out exactly that kind of authoritarian inquiry of which the patient complains. The discourse doubles back on itself and stops. What does it say but, "Very well, you caught me and you were right; now, let's get back to working on you." Why not wonder how they got into that subtle coercion? How does it match with other aspects of the patient's life? What was called out in the therapist? Let us suppose the patient was always very submissive to his father's opinions. That does not explain why the therapist coerced him. Or, if the therapist has that tendency, it does not explain why he did it with this patient, or why he is so astonished to be found out. Would it be unscientific to suggest that they talk about their mutual experience rather than "analyze" it?

To summarize: psychoanalysis had originally postulated a serious antinomy between word and deed. It was the "talking cure," and what was acted upon could not be spoken about, or analyzed. Classically, psychoanalysis had no real lexicon for behavior, and it befell Sullivan to introduce the operational concept of participant observation, a concept that has broadened considerably since its introduction. (See Gerald Chrzanowski for review of contributions to the participant-observation paradigm.)[15] It now encompasses a rather wide range of behaviors and perceptions on the part of the therapist. Otto Kernberg, Heinz Kohut, Hyman Muslin and Morton Gill, and Roy Schafer have recently championed more orthodox revisionisms of traditional psychoanalytic theory.[16]

Transference, as a concept, makes very little sense if one conceptualizes the patient as only talking or fantasying in the field of an inactive blank-screen analyst. It is a denial of the operational reality that communication (if not speech) always goes on and that the transference arena is a subtle, ongoing dialogic discourse between the two participants even when the therapist is totally silent.

Linguistic concepts make it possible to view language as more than speech and much less than the total field of semiotic communication. From this viewpoint action, or behavior, *is* a language that will be a precise transform of the speech. What the patient and the therapist talk about will be simultaneously shown or played out between them. To reiterate: *the power of psychoanalysis may well depend on what is said about what is done.* This is a continuous, integral part of the therapy, not an intermittent artifact of bad therapy. Ludwig Wittgenstein said, "What can be shown cannot be said," by which I suspect he meant that talk and action are really different modalities, parallel but not interchangeable. Therefore, I am not suggesting that the therapist match his behavior to what he hears by being the good father or stern father or whatever. The interaction must be as authentic and perplexing an aspect of the total discourse as is speech. I don't think it is ultimately possible to know why change occurs, but I feel reasonably sure change is not a consequence of the communication of meaning alone. The linguistically alert therapist, by paying attention to the concordance of spoken and acted language, facilitates the process even if he doesn't know exactly what it is he is doing.

The psychoanalyst—he who talks with his patients—is the person who is trying to understand and clarify an ordinary process, really most naturally performed without thinking too much about it. Cloaked in structuralist trappings, the inquiry has tones of grandeur. As Roland Barthes put it, "Once again the exploration of language, conducted by linguistics, psychoanalysis, and literature, corresponds to the exploration of the cosmos."[17] But, put in humbler terms, we are trying to figure out how we manage to put one foot in front of the other without falling on our faces in the process.

CHAPTER 9

Psychoanalysis:
Cure or Persuasion

> When [psychoanalysis] becomes an
> institution, when it is applied to so-called
> "normal subjects," it utterly ceases to be
> a conception that can be justified or
> discussed on the basis of cases; it no
> longer cures, it persuades.
> —CLAUDE LÉVI-STRAUSS

THE ACT of psychoanalysis, the praxis of therapy, follows a commonly-held algorithm. This algorithm is not derived from theoretical or metapsychological postures but is arrived at empirically. It works because it taps into an intrinsic deep structure of cognition. It contrives a game, a highly-augmented situation in which semiotic transactions can be observed and influenced. It must be emphasized that its efficacy, no different from that of other forms of propagandizing influence, depends on its resonance to deep structures of thought. It can, therefore, be used to different ends. What is cure and what is persuasion? In psychoanalysis, the danger is that the theory becomes an ideological indoctrination sui generis and the patient becomes a disciple.*

Is there a psychoanalytic cure distinct from persuasion, a unique psychoanalytic process that is something more than or, better yet, other than, the therapist's molding the patient to his particular view of man? Is the therapist's vaunted system of meanings and interpretations merely a strategy to produce the change he deems necessary? Are we involved in persuading the patient to live better without letting him know we are doing so? There has been considerable confusion throughout the history of psychoanalysis about the relationship of its means to its ends. Yet, how can one possibly do therapy without some system of beliefs, some structuring orientation; and simultaneously, how can one avoid making psychoanalysis a technique of persuasion, of eliciting change in the direction selected by the therapist?

Whether the patient is seen as victim or wrongdoer doesn't much matter. Whether the therapy proceeds along principles of Martin Buber or Machiavelli doesn't much matter. Whether the therapist is nurturing or depriving doesn't much matter. Even if the therapist exercises the greatest possible restraint, he cannot fail to see the material according to his own categories of experience and belief. It is a neo-Kantian imperative. There is no psychoanalytic neutrality, be the patient upright or horizontal, be the therapist garrulous or silent as the grave. If the therapist knows where the therapy should go and what the outcome should be, it is, *pari passu*, ideological and unavoidably persuasive. One may have a metapsychology that holds that the patient has been mystified by family experience. The goal of therapy becomes to lift the mystification, to let

---

*I would define ideology as a system of beliefs that explains the past, defines the present, and predicts the future. Lévi-Strauss put it very nicely when he said that a myth is a "machine for the suppression of time." Ideologies, too, take out of life all the unpredictables, contingencies, and tendency to novelty. Newtonian clockwork predictability reigns.

the patient see that he has learned not to "know what he knows he knows." But I cannot see this as an emergent process. It is ideological conversion, no matter what emphasis is put on transference. It is in the service of directed change; that is, cure follows the patient's acceptance of the therapist's truth.

Technique is the rhetoric of this process. Khan has said facetiously that we obtain the patient's truth so that we can tell him the metatruth.[1] Resistances to truth (proper meaning) are worked through, analyzed. This often becomes a series of metacommunicational ploys much as Jay Haley has described.[2] Moreover, it has been claimed that manipulation of the patient or of the family milieu is justifiable in terms of therapeutic ends. It is indeed this element of unabashed manipulation that makes some family therapy seem uncomfortably fascistic to the analytic therapist struggling to be neutral. The family therapist makes the decision about what constitutes relevant living and pushes the patient toward it. At the other end of the continuum, one finds those therapists who feel that such direction is a serious political contaminant to the therapy process; that the therapist must guard against even unconsciously coloring the therapy with what he thinks matters. And, of course, there has been a great deal of protest about the tendency of some therapists to politicize improvement, to define it in terms of their own value systems.

How, then, can a therapist maintain neutrality? In this sense, what actually defines participant observation? Is it possible to be an observer of a process in which one is a participant? Is there something operationally paradoxical in this concept? To restate the original question, is there a therapy independent of the therapist's beliefs? Is it possible to do therapy without subtly persuading the patient to believe what you believe? What it comes to is that unless the method of arriving at the truth is at least as relevant as the truth arrived at, then, I would claim, one is pressing ideology. In other words, *unless one ex-*

amines the method by which one arrives at the truth and treats that as having an independent validity, separate from the truth arrived at, then one simply is indoctrinating the patient.

The schism in perspective on cure or persuasion may be seen in the following exegesis of a book by Paul Dewald, *The Psychoanalytic Process: A Case Illustration.* [3] The patient he describes is a twenty-six-year-old woman suffering from a variety of anxiety symptoms, phobic avoidances, and jealous preoccupations. It is clear that Dr. Dewald sees as the goal of therapy with this woman the elucidation of her irrationality; that is, her oedipal fantasies, her wish for a penis, and her deeper, pre-oedipal rage at the mother. The fantasies arrive fulsomely, the patient leaves presumably cured, and Dr. Dewald, satisfied with the outcome, indulges himself in a little post-termination sentimentality, which, he hastens to assure us, he will expose to self-analysis. Very good.

I think the therapy is a miscarriage. I will try to show why I think so, but I must emphasize that I would agree that the patient showed some improvement, largely because the intrinsic good intention, decency, and integrity of the therapist permitted her to utilize her own personality resources. I see her problem as the attempt of an angry, depressed, and devaluated woman to break free from a family and marital situation that is driving her under, but which she cannot identify as destructive because she is too good a little girl and too afraid to lose her support systems. She comes into therapy complaining of her submission and leaves properly submissive, understanding that her husband loves her and that she can't have a penis. She leaves admitting that she is not really happy but is resigned to her "reality," which she now sees as benign and nurturant. There is not a single real, concrete complaint about the quality of her life, her marriage, her husband's shortcomings.

To go into detail, the opening gambit of therapy is simply

incredible. Look—she is screened by Dr. Dewald at his psycho-analytic clinic. She wants clinic therapy because there is no way she and her husband can pay for private therapy without great hardship. She waits *nine months* for a decision to be made. Then she is turned down! We are not told why. Why would a clinic refuse a potential patient screened positively by its di-rector? I've directed a clinic, and, I must say, I would be furi-ous. At any rate, Dr. Dewald then has the social worker, who has been holding the fort, inform the patient that *if* she can pay his fee, he has time. The patient agrees, and therapy be-gins. He never discusses fees with her directly, no one discusses the hardship issue before therapy begins, and no one takes up with her how it is possible that the director himself is taking her on when the clinic sees her as unsuitable. Nor is it clear why he is taping sessions or taking such copious notes. This entire opening gambit is never discussed again, never taken up with her; it is considered somehow extraneous to the therapy. When she comes in the first few sessions, blind with rage, it is interpreted as a carry-over from the previous therapy, or anxi-ety about getting started with a *real* analyst, not a social worker or psychotherapist.

The die is cast. It is clear to the patient on some denied level that she is back in the old soup; she will have to submit or be broken. As she rages on, dreaming, associating, Dr. Dewald pursues his inexorable path. The patient learns which fantasies are de rigeur and supplies them, screaming and kicking (or, rather, *gagging*) every foot of the way. She eroticizes the fanta-sies in what I would consider a desperate attempt to make the submission palatable, to sugar-coat the bitter pill (or, in Dr. Dewald's imagery, his semen, which she repeatedly refers to in oral-incorporative fellatio fantasies). She knows what she is going to have to swallow.

The detail is endless and would require a page-by-page annotation, but just to use a few examples: in session two the patient says, "I'm afraid that you'll think that I'm terrible if I tell you these things."

Dr. D.: "If I suggest to you that for the purpose of analysis you let down your usual barriers and say everything that comes into your mind, then what right do I have to have a reaction if you do just that? We'll stop here for today." What he says, in a starchy, authoritarian way, is, Don't worry about me. I'm a pro, and I won't have any reaction to you. You can trust me . . . That is his claim throughout the treatment. But he colludes with her feeling that what *he* thinks of her really matters, not what she thinks of herself.

I'd rather say to a patient, "Why do you care so much what *I* think? I could be wrong." Also, is he claiming that he never has a negative reaction to something a patient tells him? And, third, does he claim that his reassurance should make it alright for her? In short, he says to her: the issue here is your terrible fantasies, that's all that they are, they won't affect me, and they have no relationship to real experience. But I think that the patient needs the reassurance that she may be seeing something clearly, that she can stand up to the therapist, be angry, even force a concession without being killed for it.

Session three: she says, I feel hostile toward you, and I know I'm not going to get anywhere until I get it out (read: "get rid of it"). She goes on to berate him. He says, "What's the detail?" (always at the point where, if he fell silent, she would get angrier). Finally she says, I need you and cannot afford to show my hostility. Again he insists, Not *me!* She makes a submissive childhood association about her father teaching her to drive, and he says, "So we can see how hard it is for you to accept this basic idea of analysis."

When he wants fantasy he asks, "What's the detail?" When he wants submission, he repeats her last line: to wit, she says,

"My feeling is that you expect me to be perfect." He says, "Your feeling is that I expect you to be perfect here. What comes to your mind?" (clearly establishing that this is *her* distortion). But maybe it isn't. After all, he wrote her up in detail, with postsession notes. I cannot believe that he does so for every patient. So why for her?

Was he planning in advance to publish an account of a complete analysis? If so, maybe she damn well had to be perfect, had to work out the way he wanted. And what better patient for that than one who owes you one, is grateful for therapy proffered over the rejection of the clinic? Can you imagine taking copious notes, paying for two years of word-for-word transcriptions, and *then* having the therapy flop?

In session forty-seven, she's still struggling with her rage toward this superior man who is requiring that she submit. She says, "I just haven't got the strength to hate you." In session forty-eight she has a dream:

In the dream I'm feminine and cuddly and soft and warm and loving. I was never accepted by my father this way as a child, but now I feel as if you may accept me. In the dream we are in the playpen [oh, shades of Freud—defender of the transference!], and it was in Evanston and all us girls were there. We were dressed up kind of frilly, and there were people looking in at us, and the men were in tuxedos. I was laying on the floor, and I had no pants on, and I kept wondering what the men would think.

As an addendum: she says, "Before this, when I used to dream that I was naked, I'd feel embarrassed because I was missing a penis, and I would want to run and hide away." His next response is: "What comes to mind about this feeling that I might accept you as feminine and soft and loving?" Now, in anybody's book, that is a directing query! She is clearly told which part of the dream to pick up on. Then he says, "You cut something short there" [sic!]. From there, he leads her to the penis envy. She gets upset, of course (that's resistance, so he must be right). Why not wonder why the women are little girls in a playpen and the men are grown-up and in tuxedos? Why are the little girls exposed and embarrassed? Penis envy, my foot! Shortly thereafter, the patient burst out in a tirade: "I'm in a world of woman-haters, and they all laugh at a woman because she *is* a woman. . . . I wonder if you are a woman-hater, too." Isn't that the simplest, most economical interpretation of the dream? Occam's razor, the principle in philosophy of using the most economical explanation, is not for Dr. Dewald. He wields a different razor: he sees her diatribe, in his postsession annotation, as a transference distortion, that "I want her to be a boy, accompanied by multiple examples of negation in regard to her phallic strivings, her sense of inferiority in being a girl and her projection of this in the transference and in her general feelings about men."

This woman was sexually molested as a child by an uncle. Paradoxically, what is left from that kind of experience is a feeling of great power as an object of desire, and great powerlessness as an autonomous person. Attractive women in this society can feel that without an explicit childhood seduction; that is, the power to arouse but not influence. The patient is cynically and totally convinced that all men, including the therapist, are seducible. Yet, she is powerless to get any man *really* to attend to her. This is a typical narcissistic dilemma. The child is of great interest and value to the parents as an object of admiration, ambition, or desire but of no interest whatever as a person, separate and imperfect. I would have liked to see her come into touch with some of this as a real problem for women and, for her, a problem specifically augmented by the real nature of her husband, her parents, and her uncle, the seducer; and as complicated in therapy by her real interaction with the therapist—a real man, in a real institute, having real problems with his own presuppositions, which derive from his real age, his real sociocultural experience, and his real, particular psychoanalytic training.

This woman talks about her reluctance to perform fellatio on her husband. Dr. D. presents an elaborate exegesis of why she equates mouth and vagina, her fantasies of oral incorporation of the penis, pregnancy as swallowing the baby, and the fantasy of eating the uncle's penis as representing her wish to have a penis of her own. The patient ecstatically responds, "That's the only reason I've come here. It's finally dawned on me!" Dr. D. does not wonder about her sudden enthusiasm for his interpretations as a possible reenactment (acting-in) of the issue with him. She follows up with, "For twenty-seven years I've been thinking that somehow I'll get a penis! And now I know that I'm not going to: I feel like hell and that the world is against me and that I got a raw deal. I hate them all!" In the end she swallows it to the hilt. That kind of enthusiasm for an interpretation should seem a little suspicious, even to as doctrinaire a therapist as Dr. Dewald.

Later she says, "I have the feeling that I'm a woman and that I'm proud of my body. You're a goddam stupid man, so I can never do it, and I hate you! I will always hate you!" Much of the rest of each session deals with her attempts to explicate her rage at being a woman among men and her attempts to come to terms with her mother and to find some tenable female identification. She hates her mother and rejects that version of femininity, sees her reflection in the man's eyes as a mere object of desire, and sees no way out.

To the credit of the therapy, she is free to ventilate and formulate her rage. But she does not get any validation of it as a real response to real events in a real life. Is that necessary? For Dr. Dewald it is not, since the fantasies have a life of their own. For me it is vital, since I would want the patient to leave therapy not only feeling different but equipped differently; that is, being more competent to control her own life and to change it.

By the twenty-fourth month the patient is anticipating leaving: "All I have to do is accept it, and accept the fact that Tom loves me and that there is absolutely nothing wrong with me. Thinking like that really bothers me. I'm thinking that. . . . there's nothing here for me. . . . I have nothing to hate now because all that I hated is in the past." She leaves finally with some very ambiguous statements about her feelings. She feels grown-up and ready to go, but sad to leave. That's fine, but she also sounds as though she has rejected, along with her neurosis, any chance of contacting her authentic self. I repeat, I think it is a failure.

The therapist has an entire set of premises about what kind of material must be forthcoming and what the resolution must be. The patient must come into contact with noxious fantasy systems that are polluting her life. Dr. Dewald knows exactly what material is to be forthcoming, the only question being the depth of the patient's disturbance; that is, is it oedipal or pre-oedipal? That, however, is expected to emerge in the course of the therapy. In all of Dr. Dewald's postsession annotational notes, it is striking how little interest or belief he shows in the patient's uniqueness. There is no sense that something unexpected might emerge or that the material might turn in some unpredicted direction. We learn virtually nothing about her, her friends, her interests, her dreams of success. One gets no feeling for who this woman really is. It is as in biology: the inside of animals is always colorless and always the same—one liver, two lungs, and so forth. It is on the outside that the uniqueness resides—in feathers, coloring, details of appearance. Dr. Dewald's view of psychoanalysis reduces people to their commonly-held interior anatomy. I would have preferred to learn something about his patient's surface. I think that it is the limitations of this classical view of therapy that led to the object-relations schism and the interpersonal school of Sullivan and his followers. Never does Dr. Dewald say to himself, "Who would have thought?" It is always, "Aha! Now we are arriving at this or that level." He knows where the psychoanalysis is going; he makes mistakes only when a countertransference gets in the way. Otherwise, the patient is played like an organ console; stops are pulled out, adjusted. If you will forgive a double entendre—Dr. Dewald is the master organist!

All this plays into the patient's narcissistic experience. Again she is an object of interest and desire, but in no way is she a unique person. I think it might be necessary to be curious about her and not her dynamics, to not understand her until she emerges with the necessary self-revelations, and to expect that at the end of therapy she will have changed her life, her way of relating to others, her expectations and understanding of others, and not simply have come to terms with her dynamics, given up her infantile expectations. Therapy, in Dewald's terms, is an exercise in renunciation. I would prefer it to be an exercise in self-realization. This is, of course, easy to say and might sound self-serving and self-indulgent. There are, however, different disciplines involved: the classical therapist ties himself to the mast; the interpersonalist commits himself to the stream. That there may be a legitimate and somewhat acrimonious difference of opinion here is evident.*

---

*See Samuel Lipton's article on the Dewald book for a critique which, while done from a different theoretical perspective, presents much the same conclusion.[4]

CHAPTER 10

The Moral Posture:

Sincerity or Authenticity

The way to use life is to do nothing
through acting; the way to use life is to
do everything through being.
                              —LAOTZU

HERMES, the messenger of the Olympian gods, not only delivered messages to humans but put them into human language—hence, *hermeneutics,* the science of interpretation. Psychoanalysis can be seen as a hermeneutic act with interpretation viewed as a thrust toward a covered truth, or as a language-act, with interpretation seeking to explicate the nature of relationships. The idea that there is a hidden truth is not limited to Freudian psychoanalysis; it is equally evident, for example, in Erich Fromm, where the "forgotten language" of dreams reveals a hidden wisdom.[1]

This position proliferates a series of antinomies: shallow/deep, manifest/latent, superficial/profound. Underneath the world of appearances there is a Truth, which must be sought and identified. When Freud's sons were at the battle front in World War I, he dreamed that one, Martin, had been killed. Freud wrote to Jones that the dreams must refer to his "envy of their youth."[2] There *must be* a hidden meaning; the obvious and reasonable concern is not enough. If there is no hidden (latent) meaning, what becomes of the theory?

Some part of the patient is allied with this quest for meaning. Messages are slipped past the censor; slips, parapraxes, associations, and dreams are glimpses of hidden truth. The message-in-the-bottle (as Walker Percy called it) metaphor prevails. Truth, like the Holy Grail, is revealed to the parfait psychoanalyst, one who is without fault—sincere. If the Truth arrived at "works"; that is, if the patient changes, it tautologically reinforces the therapist's belief in his hermeneutics. Thus, as I have suggested, therapy becomes a very powerful rhetoric, a persuasion to change in the direction valued by the therapist, who may not suspect that the change occurred, not necessarily because it was "right," but because the therapy taps into a deep linguistic structure. It is as though a huckster, using powerful subliminal influencing techniques to sell a particular brand of toothpaste, succeeded, and then decided that the successful sale must prove the superiority of his product, not his propaganda. Family therapists have been fascinated by the work of Milton Erickson, a hypnotist, who is extraordinarily facile at tuning in on, and potentiating, marginal semiotic cues. Patients can be changed, against their will, or, at least, without their conscious collaboration.[3] What, then, if therapeutic effectiveness depends not on the hermeneutic truth but the algorithm, the process; even worse, what if the vaunted change, the result of the process, is only that—change—not necessarily for better or for worse? If cure can become ideological indoctrination, how does the therapist know if he is right? The success of a particular theoretical set cannot be used to prove its correctness; one can only say that the therapist is effective in getting his truth acknowledged.

Yet, it is undeniable that clinical material often does sound as if someone living inside the patient were trying to slip us the Truth. One patient in his forties dreams that there is an elephant living in his parents' apartment. The elephant is very considerate; he is house-trained, and only occasionally does he soil the rug. He tries very hard not to knock over the walls. But he is an elephant; he never forgets an abuse!

Surely, this dream is transparent. Who is dreaming it? Can this blatant manifest content have slipped past a censor? If so, why is it not more disguised? Does the patient not know what this dream refers to? Of course, he knows that the dream refers to him in his parents' home, that the elephant is hunkered down, constrained, trying not to make trouble, but holding on to and savoring every injustice. It would be consoling to stop the inquiry at this point, because if one continues, the possibilities begin to expand exponentially. Is it a statement about his relationship with the therapist? Why did he dream it now? Does he really think he is that powerful? How could he knock over the walls? Perhaps by not getting better. If one does not look for an underlying unifying truth, then ambiguity increases.

The therapist recalls that he is often in this predicament with this man; he is enchanted and interested in material that seems so clear and naïve as about to reveal to him the Truth (even though he doesn't believe in the Truth). Somehow, the clarity dissipates, leaving him stranded and annoyed—stranded: didn't the patient some time ago dream of having a large white shark in a tub in his office with just enough water to keep the shark alive? Hadn't the "white shark" raised the association to the White Institute, the therapist's affiliation? Hadn't the question of negative transference been raised at that time? Hadn't the patient congratulated the therapist on his cleverness in detecting the "white shark" play of words? And so it goes.

In the pursuit of the dream, the dream is replayed with the therapist. If the patient is not sending us a message, how can one explain the apparent coherence of the dream? I suspect it lies in the intrinsic nature of cognitive process, which I shall take up in the section on neuropsychology. One might consider that although an Apache tracker can reconstruct an entire history of a buffalo from his droppings, it does not follow that the buffalo endorses that purpose.

If one sees psychoanalysis as a language-act, a different set of postulates emerges. There is no hidden truth to be pursued through a vertical landscape. There is only increasing pattern and complexity, the "infinite regress" referred to in chapter 8. Events in the therapy spread, expanding concentric circles of inquiry like pebbles dropped into a pond, coalescing, overlapping, forming moiré patterns in perception. This metaphor may seem a poor alternative to the clarity of the Freudian linearity. But, as I shall cover later in more detail, it may be close to the way the brain/mind really works. At any rate, instead of antinomy, the interpersonalist has paradox. Instead of *sincerity,* he has *authenticity* and the recognition that persuasion and indoctrination can only be avoided if the therapist has no goals for the patient and no conviction about how he or she should live. Ambiguity is not tolerated as a way station to truth but is celebrated as the human state. The patient then has difficult and real choices to make: imperfect solutions in an imperfect world.

The interpersonal therapist does not claim neutrality and does not strive toward it. Instead of sincerity (literally, being without stain), the interpersonalist works toward authenticity, which embraces an entirely different concept. From the Greek *authentikos,* it means to be the author of one's own acts and, oddly enough (as Webster's dictionary informs us), to be a murderer! The Homeric Greeks considered man to be directed by the gods. Behind every hero stood a god. To kill at the behest of the god was fine; to do it on one's own initiative was murder. One was not supposed to think for oneself. The internalized effort to be one's best is replaced by the interpersonal effort to be, with others, oneself, with all one's imperfections and shortcomings. Authenticity tries to match being and action; sincerity tries to perfect being and, consequently, action. The authentic therapist, then, takes responsibility into his own hands. If he is right, he is right; if he is wrong, he is wrong. He cannot blame it on the patient's "resistance" or "borderline pathology" or a premature "too deep" interpretation.*

In the safety and security of the therapeutic "playground" (in Freud's term), the patient learns either that his fantasies are not real and need not control his life, or, from my point of view, that in interaction with another imperfect person he can acquire the skills necessary to discriminate, identify, and influence the other—thus, the need for "good enough" therapists, not ideal therapists. Maturity emerges not as a learned experience but as a by-product of a sense of power and control of one's own life. The patient, too, takes an authentic risk. He learns that to trust someone is not an easy thing, that a real disappointment is possible and remains a risk even with the acquisition of increased interpersonal awareness. To live is to take your life in your hands!

To put it rather reductively, one might apply these different therapeutic models to Freud's famous case of Little Hans, the boy who was afraid of being bitten by a horse. A directive, relationship psychotherapist would hold him by the hand, have

---

*See Lionel Trilling, *Sincerity and Authenticity,* for a most lucid presentation of this theme.[4]

him pat the horse: "See, nice horsey won't bite." Trust of the therapist leads to risk taking and reassurance. Little Hans learns to ride. The classical analytic approach puts Little Hans on the couch or in the playroom. When he understands that his fear of horses is a displacement of his fear of the castrating father, he will be free to pat the horse or not. The therapist couldn't care less. It is understood that Little Hans's father was a nice guy; the fantasy is distortion "driven" by libido or, perhaps these days, anxiety. In the interpersonal approach, Little Hans is led to see that his father is *not* necessarily such a nice guy. His uneasiness is appropriate. When Little Hans becomes more competent to handle his family, perhaps with the aid of a family therapist's intervention, when he feels safe, he will pat the horse. He will pat the horse because he has learned how to judge what is safe, and how to trust his own judgment. It doesn't pay to be too trusting of the helper or the horse. After all, some horses, like some people, do bite.

Shouts of "Simplistic! Nihilism!" can be heard from the audience. But the interpersonalist approach is not a denial of values or of moral or even immoral choices. Nor is it skepticism. It simply says that psychoanalysis may not answer questions, only raise them, and leave the answers to the patient. A neurotic, it has been said, is a person who knows only one way to do something, and that way doesn't work. One might well add, but still, it is better than something else. A neurotic solution is highly redundant; that is, it always works the same way. Nothing works like neurotic solutions, and this consistency of effect is immensely reassuring to a frightened and disabled person—at least things won't get worse. I do not think that it is the mission of the analyst to provide the patient with a better way to that one thing. One hope's that the patient, with augmented semiotic skills and with a fuller and richer grasp of the complexity of his life as lived with his parents, with colleagues, and in society, will be freer to make choices and to assume the responsibility of those choices. The psychoanalytic algorithm is the prototype of a more creative problem solving.

Many people enter therapy complaining of difficulties they trust will be gone by the time they leave. They may wish, for example, to be "intimate" with someone. They hope that when their oedipal or pre-oedipal difficulties are resolved they will spontaneously discover this desideratum with their mates or friends. The positive transfer may be the desperate hope that the therapist (superior being) has achieved what the patient wishes for himself. Or, if they come to interpersonalists, they hope to learn how to feel closeness. I would prefer that patients leave therapy committed to the lifetime pursuit of dialogue, with the recognition that "intimacy" may be more the epiphany of hard work at living than a directed goal.

The conversion from sincerity to authenticity is seen with some frequency in patients; a similar conversion in a therapist is a less-observed phenomenon. The following case example is from material presented by a British Kleinian, Donald Meltzer,[5] in an article titled "Routine and Inspired Interpretations." It is of particular interest because of two distinct levels of transaction. The first is the absolute inability of the therapist, at first bound to his theory, to see the simple facts of his relationship to the patient as reflected in a dream. And the second level is the therapist's inspired efforts to transcend his theoretical position and engage the patient in an authentic process. The patient has a dream:

He and the analyst seem to be sharing a hotel room which is overlooked by rooftops filled with people. At one point the analyst seems to be squatting over the patient, saying something like, "in fact you have never actually seen my anus." The patient felt a mixture of intense emotions. On the one hand he felt embarrassed that the people across the way would surely see this as a homosexual relationship. But even more acute was a feeling of triumph over the analyst, who was apparently quite unaware that behind him was a mirror which enabled the patient to look directly between his buttocks. These appeared huge and muscular, like a Japanese wrestler's.

This dream was analyzed totally without reference to current reality. The usual childhood associations and transferential associations follow. The therapist fails to connect the dream with the obvious fact that he is reading a paper based on the case to the British Psychoanalytic Society (where it was received in a "friendly but uneasy way"), that this is the audience watching in the dream, that the therapist's "ass is hanging out," that he doesn't know it but the patient does, that the patient and therapist are collaborating in some collusive way that the British Psychoanalytic Society might be uneasy about, and that the patient has mixed feelings about his case material being used in a battle the therapist may be having with his colleagues.

Does this sound extreme? Later in the article we are told that "the patient himself heard about it (the case presentation) through a friend [sic!], realized it was about him, and asked to read it. I agreed; he was pleased with it and found that its content corresponded to his recollection—and all Hell broke loose! He gave up his career, left his wife, gave over to a 'latent perversion,' failed to attend sessions, did not pay his bills and lost most of his friends." Later material (yes, the therapy did continue for several more years) revealed the patient's childhood devotion to secretly sucking his thumb; this man was a master at keeping sly secrets.

The dream not only told what was happening but foretold what *would* happen. Attending to what the patient said in the dream would have alerted the therapist to the patient's awareness of the forthcoming presentation and would have opened up the exploration of the patient's collusive, secret setting-up of the therapist; but only as an exploration of the patient's participation. To include the therapist would have evoked an authentic risk, since the therapist did not really know what he was doing. But it would appear to be his wish to expose himself in some combative way to the conservative psychoanalytic society. Was he using the patient to work through his own rebelliousness?

At this point, the therapy sounds like an opéra bouffe. All is in disarray. But the therapist does an interesting and courageous thing. He gives up knowing without giving up the therapy. He and the patient spend several more years sorting it all out, and a second recovery occurs which he suspects, but *is not sure,* may be more authentic. He stops guiding the patient and becomes a covoyager. I think he comes out as changed as the patient. The final form of the paper says, "I am *letting* my ass hang out." "I don't know," the therapist says, and I quote, "whether this has been a successful analysis or a catastrophe . . . but it has had a profound influence on my own development." In his own somewhat floridly literary concept, he stops playing Virgil, the guide to the patient's Dante, and becomes, instead, Daedalus to his Leopold Bloom, a fellow wanderer in the double-entendre maze.

So, in the end, we can say that the dream says as much about the therapist and his goals and development as it does about the patient. Remember that this was the *patient's* dream. Certainly one must agree that his unconscious grasp of events, real events, was remarkable. I do not believe that this example is extreme or unusual. The literature is chock-full of examples of obvious interpersonal realities sacrificed to procrustean theoretical positions. It is, unfortunately, less full of such courageously authentic voyages.

CHAPTER 11

Models of the Mind:
Landscape or Network

No problem is too difficult to be solved
by a theoretician.
                    —Sufi saying

IT MIGHT SEEM from the clinical material presented that
I am setting up a straw man, holding the metapsychology responsible for its misapplication. But, if the theory does not dictate its ends, it is captive and can be put to any use the therapist
desires. It loses its relevance as a therapeutic instrument, let
alone as an abstract truth. Unquestionably, excellent therapy
is done by therapists using the most restrictive sets; but success
depends on the therapist's artistry, his ability to maneuver intuitively within the constraints of his system. It also depends on
the flexibility and resiliency of our underesteemed collaborator,
the patient, who often fleshes out a therapy, quietly elaborating
those dimensions of relationships that the therapist ignores.
Sometimes a friend or family member is utilized as
alter-therapist; other times the interplay is so subtle that the
therapist is unaware that he is engaged in far more interaction

than he reports. Any interpretive system that fails to see that the interpreter *is* his interpretation remains, in my view, too static to be effective.

Criticism about the nature and limits of Freudian metapsychology have been raised, within the loose Freudian enclave, by those Alvin Frank has called "the reformers"—namely, Schafer, Robert Holt, Melanie Klein, and Gill.[1] Still, the criticism never jumps the fence, never leaves the reservation. Schafer, whose "action language" seems most like a radical departure from Freudian drive theory, still protests that repetition in therapy is "an enactment or re-enactment of certain wishful, conflictual, and frightening infantile situations, such as the primal scene, that unconsciously have continued to be treated as real and current . . ."[2] Muslin and Gill, discussing the Dora case, agree that "deviations from an ideally neutral framework" interfere with therapy, although they disagree with Langs as to whether the deviation per se or the failure to interpret the deviation is the problem.[3] In spite of the simulation of congruence, there are clearly different gods being worshiped in different pantheons.

It is interesting to contrast this traditional concern with the issues of distortion and therapist neutrality with the case of Sabina Spielrein, as presented in Aldo Carotenuto's book *A Secret Symmetry.*[4] There, an apparently psychotic young woman becomes Jung's patient and is embroiled in an affair with him. There is no issue of distortion. For once, we have a fait accompli. She writes to Freud, Freud writes to Jung. Jung admits that he has made a mess of it. There is a bizarre exchange of letters between Jung and Sabina's parents, who cannot but remain grateful to him for her recovery from a disastrous collapse. Freud doesn't really know what to do. He tries tactfully and helpfully to mediate, largely through a long correspondence with Sabina. She ends up a psychoanalyst and a significant contributor to the literature.

Models of the Mind: Landscape or Network

This account is very likely the worst donnybrook in the psychoanalytic literature; and yet, Sabina's case worked out far better than that of poor Dora, who, in spite of Freud's most meticulous and ethical efforts, was later described by Felix Deutsch as a therapeutic catastrophe.[5] How can one account for such an odd alchemy of gold into disaster and disaster into gold? I suspect it was because, for Sabina Spielrein, *no one denied her reality.* Jung had the decency not to discredit her, which would have been easy enough to do. He could have accused her of hallucinating, and sealed her certain fate. The entire scenario is striking for its authenticity: no one, Freud included, quite knew what to do. They had the tact and decency not to "analyze" her motives, and the complicated matrix was acknowledged by all. Perhaps the authenticity was the curative element.

The thesis, then, is that psychoanalysis works not because of what it says but how it proceeds, throwing an ever-widening seine of inquiry that is of a semiotic nature. The uniqueness of psychoanalysis lies in its particular framing, which permits the participants to use themselves in an infinite regress of meta-communications about the data the patient presents about his or her life. The therapist's particular explanatory system is only a metaphor, a way of pulling things together, of parenthesizing data. It is neither intrinsically correct nor incorrect but, rather, a commentary on the interactional field. But since each commentary is a selection of position, however inadvertent an attitude about what is being told by the patient, every interpretation becomes an interaction.

Why should a process that simply expands data, enriches pattern, work? If one keeps extending the field of inquiry, encompassing wider and wider vistas of interaction, one might expect the therapy to wallow finally in chaos. If the therapist does not order and organize and clarify, how can the patient?

Two different models of the mind inform the question. The

first, the traditional psychoanalytic model, is essentially vertical, each layer suppressing and modulating the function of the
strata beneath. The second model is lateral and spatial; instead
of levels of hierarchical suppression, there is a collated network
of patterned information. Both these views reflect the neuropsychological paradigm of their times.

In turn-of-the-century neurology, it was believed that there
existed a stratification of neurological functioning. From comparative neurology it was known that as new areas of the brain
developed, they exerted control over the lower areas by a process of suppression. That is to say, the oldest part of the brain,
the brain stem, was controlled and suppressed by the newer
part of brain, the cortex. (The Papez-MacLean theory of brain
evolution is an elaboration of this thesis.)[6] Ordinarily, move-
ments that are initiated in and controlled by the brain stem
are very gross and tremulous. The function of higher senses
is to smooth out, control, and modulate these more primitive
operations. In a brain lesion—say, arteriosclerosis, where cortical function is lost—the tremor *emerges* as cortical supervision,
and control of the lower brain is lost. Thus, the tremor of par-
kinsonism is a release phenomenon. The notion of brain hierarchy, then, came out of comparative neuroanatomy and neuro-
physiology, and also out of the prevalent notion of Darwinian
evolution. Freud, for example, believed that the site of emotion
was developmentally in the rhinencephalon, a large brain area
that in lower animals serves the sense of smell.

Freud developed an elaborate hypothesis of how evolutionary change to upright posture shifted the significance of
the sense of smell. As Sulloway noted, Freud's heavy leaning
on what, from our contemporary perspective, seems like
Fliess's bizarre ruminations about the nose-sex connection
was not so odd in its social context. An American laryngolo-
gist, John MacKenzie, had given credibility to Fliess's claims,

and there was a well-reputed theory of "primal-smell" advanced by the German biologist and philosopher Ernst Haeckel. None other than the highly esteemed Richard von Krafft-Ebing had given this hypothesis his imprimatur.[7]

It's not difficult to see how, from this stratified topological model of the brain, with the premise of suppression of one layer by the layer above it, Freud's model of psychological functioning would emerge. The deepest layer is the most primitive and the most turbulent, with the layers above smoothing out and modulating and socializing the activity of the lower layers. Freud saw civilization as an outgrowth of the complex evolutionary development of the brain. He therefore saw the higher levels of the brain functioning to maintain civilization in the individual. Concepts like "primary" and "secondary" modes of thought and Silvano Arieti's application of "paleological" thinking all imply the same idea: that there are deeper and more superficial levels of the brain, that the deeper levels are cruder, more unmanageable, and less civilized, and require the upper levels to modulate and control them.[8] The function of the therapist, then, must be, in some way, to reinforce the socializing aspects of the brain apparatus.

It is not that this view of the brain is incorrect or naïve. It is simply one perspective on brain physiology and neuroanatomy, and it is entirely correct. Indeed, the concept of constraining hierarchical organization is the basis of Paul MacLean's thesis and Arthur Koestler's concept of a lethal "design error" in the brain.[9] However, current scientific perspective is shifting to a new paradigm—what Ludwig Von Bertalaffny called the *organismic* perspective.[10] This viewpoint moves away from the Darwinism that prevailed previously, away from an interest in the evolutionary development of layers, more toward an interest in holism, the way things function as totalities. Rather than the topological localization, hierarchal layering, and suppression of the traditional view of neurological functioning, there is now a different perspective, based on three factors.

1. *Holistic Functioning:* The entire brain is involved in every neurological function. Although it is true that a lesion in certain parts of the cortex—for example, Broca's area, which controls speech—will produce a neurological defect, apparently additional lesions in other specific parts of the brain will cause the malfunction to disappear. In other words, what in the old model were thought to be specific topological locations for function are now seen as only important points in a three-dimensional network of connections that encompass the entire brain.

2. *Interference Patterns:* Instead of a hierarchy of control, there is substituted a concept from modern communication theory in which this massive flow of input data coming from different parts of the brain, and received through different sensory modalities, produces in the brain a patterning of neurological impulse that can be sustained either momentarily or, through neuropharmacological processes, converted into a memory trace.

3. *Replication:* The concept of cortical function as suppression is replaced by a concept of cortical functioning as enlarging, enriching, or replicating of these interference patterns. The brain, then, is seen as a *three-dimensional space* that can maintain and project certain configurations.

It must be reemphasized that these two essential models of brain functioning are noncompeting versions of the truth. They are different paradigmatic sets attempting to deal with clinical phenomona.

If we ask ourselves, How do creative people manage to confront complexity without a helper, a striking homology to the second model emerges. In Koestler's "bisociating," Jacob Getzel's, Philip Jackson's, and Liam Hudson's "divergent/

convergent thinking," the "lateral thinking" of Edward De Bono, Jay Ogilvy's "multi-dimensional man," all different perspectives on the creative process, certain consistent patterns emerge.*

The first is that chaos is comfortably tolerated and even experienced as stimulating. The second is that paradox is equally tolerated and, indeed, is utilized as a mode of perception. Third, some variety of lateral, rather than vertical, thought is used. Connections are made metonymically or metaphorically; that is, the mind moves "sideways," scanning intuitively over patterns and searching for simultaneous fit, regardless of logical or formal connection. Vertical thinking is logical, reductive, analytical, sequential. Free associative rambling is of the lateral type, and focused depth interpretations are vertical. Vertical thinking is a way of parenthesizing—putting into brackets and containing discursive lateral associations.

Although, as psychoanalysts, we aspire to be scientists, not artists, there is some comfort in the idea that we may be catalyzing a creative agency in the patient; being, in Masud Khan's felicitous phrase, "the servants of a process" rather than the masters of the situation.

Consider a colleague who, while attempting to work himself into a difficult yoga position, suddenly has a memory of trotting after his father to synagogue. This Proustian recall is accompanied by a very powerful mélange of feelings and is a totally new memory. What has happened? Is it something in the postural position, the stretching? Or, is it in the total experience of pursuing some painful-but-good-for-you ascetic experience? Could it be part of the therapist's transferential relationship with the yogi who is teaching him? What has been released from his unconscious? Is it a therapeutic experience: is he somehow

*I am leaning heavily on the excellent categories established by Charles Hampden-Turner.[11]

freer, or is he simply remembering another situation in which he was a good little boy doing something difficult? Perhaps it is utterly meaningless—squeezed out of him like a grunt or a popped disc.

All these explanations are viable; they are simply different views on the same matter. Even if the memory is transferential; that is, even if it comes out of the experience of again being a little boy in a learning situation with a powerful religious father, one would still have to ask, Why now, why this way? Why did it not occur in a dream? In some way the kinesthetic input to the therapist's brain (the feelings coming from his musculo-skeletal system as he strained into position) lined up or reso-nated to provoke this whole other memory output with its emo-tional load and its relevance to the present situation. Insight and change, always unpredictable, usually ineffable, seems to be less a function of clarity of purpose than some variety of informational overload.

One hopes that this permits the therapist to recognize the limitations of interpretation, particularly of content or mean-ing. There can be a relaxation of the need to know, to under-stand, to stay *ahead* of the patient. Change, it can be said, does not come out of understanding the truth, by "making one thing absolutely clear," but by "working through," which from this perspective does not mean doing the same thing over and over, but, rather, recognizing a widening series of patterns of interaction and configurations of experience—always, I must emphasize, to some end point that is never achieved. It is an examination in great detail of the *part* to expand and clarify the *whole. The therapist does not explain content; he expands awareness of patterning.* This occurs both within a specific pa-rameter of exchange (the patient's talking about his childhood, his girlfriend, his dreams, or his experience with the therapist) and in the isomorphic relationship, the harmonic variation of the same patterning as it is repeated from one parameter to another and from one session to another. Thus, the singular patternings are seen to be homologous with a larger patterning; the part reflects the whole. Insight would be not seen so much as accreted learning but as a more holistic, total reorganization of the "reality-within." All the parameters will change, simultaneously and totally and really without a rational or logical framework of explanation. The hermeneutics may be an epiphenomenon, merely a codicil to change.

The therapist becomes part of the problem to resolve it. He uses his own sense of participation as a particularly acute instrument of pattern recognition but can extrapolate from his experience to the other areas of isomorphic patterning to better understand what he is experiencing. By virtue of this activity, he is able to effect a major discontinuous transformation of the patient's patterning—insight and change result. Why does this happen? I think it is because expansion and resonance hit closest to the real neuropsychological substrate of revelation.

Interpreting or explaining superimposes a linear explanation on a complex, undelineated analogic activity. It brackets and focuses one aspect or perspective on an interactional field that is essentially, if one extends it into the social matrix, infinite. Explanation says, "Look here, settle for this aspect!" It is reductive, delineating. On the other hand, if one extends and expands patterning, permitting concentric circles of expanding data to emerge, one gets higher and higher levels of organization and the patient and therapist collaborate in a creative process, which is enriching but not necessarily clarifying. Real choices must still be made by the patient.

A patient may come into therapy because he or she cannot decide whether to leave a mate for someone else. The patient hopes that some psychodynamic formulation forthcoming will make it all clear and predicate a decision; to wit, he wishes to leave his wife because he is acting-out, is having a midlife crisis, because she was his parents' choice, or he is terrified of women in general and focusing the fear on his wife. Or, he wants to go because he needs to fulfill himself; he has sacrificed his life to being a good boy, caring for others. It has not been my experience that such decisions clarify themselves very successfully or that, when they do, the clarity persists far beyond the end of therapy.

Psychoanalysis should not be confused with soothsaying. All that therapy can do is enrich the patient's knowledge of himself, his mate, and their interaction. The decision, though, usually remains a decision, and painful choices must be made. The therapist cannot know what the patient should do from the clinical material, unless, of course, it is perfectly obvious, as it is not a wise idea for a homosexual bank president to pick up lovers in the subway toilet. That is "acting-out," which can be quite simply defined as anything that makes the therapist nervous. But then, one need not be a psychoanalyst to give that advice. Take, for example, the following dream of a man in the throes of marital indecision:

"I am standing on a ridge overlooking a beautiful vista in Central Park. It is lovely, sylvan; the colors are striking. I notice that I can see, across the park, an apartment building that overlooks the glen. I think to myself that I hope no one in the building has noticed this spot. I could hurry and buy it and develop it, if the Parks Department would be willing to sell it. I hate to see it going to waste. People bicycle by in a group. They are dressed in 'punk' clothes: garter belts, pink hair, studded jackets."

This is a man whose life has been characterized by a good deal of acquisitiveness, masked by a rather patrician diffidence. It is easy to see the dream as a hidden wisdom; he is unable to let things be, to simply enjoy beauty. He has to acquire it, own it, exploit it, profit from it. He is a "marketing" personality, in Fromm's terminology. He would be very relieved by this interpretation. It is thunderingly patriarchal; it tells him to behave himself. If it were extended to his marriage, it becomes clear that he wishes to leave only because the grass is greener on some distant vista. Who are the people in motley, the latest decadent chic? Fools?

But Central Park has been designated as "forever wild." He knows very well how bitterly any intrusion into it has been fought. Why does he pick Central Park? Why not Long Island Sound or some other prime real estate? Why is he at a distance from the lovely spot, not in it? Is he saying that it is not considered "smart" by the world to simply enjoy life, to pursue one's own pleasures, like the group of "punks" playing in the park? One must be grown-up, do only what profits one. Perhaps there is some part of him that he has never developed, never integrated into his life? Is "forever wild" necessarily good? One could elaborate endless combinations and permutations of these themes. Therapy will not show the patient a Way; many analysts would give lip service to this concept, agreeing that psychoanalysis was never intended to provide certainty. Freud, it is often said, feared that psychoanalysis, in its transit to the United States, would be bowdlerized into a benign system of uplift, promising patients happiness, togetherness, and contentment. Freud had the "Tragic View"; he understood clearly that this was neither possible nor desirable. Yet, in various clinical reports, one is struck again and again by therapists' agendas—sometimes secret, sometimes not, but always present. It is no more possible in an energic paradigm (one in which one believes in libido, drive) not to have a target than it is to fire a pistol without hitting something: force impels a target.

One might compare this certainty with Sullivan's interest in Mark Twain's *The Mysterious Stranger.* [12] It is a story of interventions in which, each time, the outcome is worse than the original disaster. To quote Helen Perry, "Sullivan seemed to use the story as a parable for psychoanalysts and psychiatrist. . . . if a change is to be made, then the person must decide for himself, for no one else has the wisdom to dictate such a change to another human being."[13]

Admittedly, all this is rather irritating. The patient comes to therapy with a difficult choice to make. He doesn't know how "neurotic" his impulses are and he wants help in making a "mature" decision. He hopes to discover that his wish to leave his marriage is infantile, or that his wish to stay is dependent. He fervently desires that, when he has in the course of the therapy discovered which it is, he will feel relieved and no longer be at odds with himself. If I am saying that he will not get that as a legitimate goal of therapy, then what does he get and how does one help?

Clinical experience suggests that when a patient has elaborated a network of perception about his childhood, his present life, his style of decision making, recognized the richness of his own associative processes, he *does* make decisions—usually satisfactory ones. But more important, since these are his decisions, he stands by them, develops and elaborates them. Any therapist who sees many patients in second (or third) treatments is struck by how many patients complete a first therapy with a series of successful decisions and personal developments but then expect to live happily ever after without misgivings or regrets. The patient clings to the secret conviction that, even if the therapist denies it, his is a Way that promises unconflicted living. These patients wish to be cured—like a side of bacon.

Psychoanalytic candidates are very happy if one tells them what is right and what is wrong about what they are doing, what is wrong with the patient, and what the desirable outcome must be. They tend to turn morose and irritable with the approach I am presenting as preferable. It is precisely the disorientation which Meltzer described in "Routine and Inspired Interpretations" (see chapter 10).

Why should the analyst know what is wrong with the patient? Clever analysts have always known that their function is paradoxical. It is the goal of the therapist to fail the patient's expectations, not meet them. *Psychoanalysis is the science of omissions:* it studies them in the patient's life and provides them in the therapist-patient relationship. The very psychoanalytic frame provides a vacuum for the patient to fill.

Psychoanalytic training tends to sustain the chimera of certainty and clear purpose. Supervision, that exemplar of the psychoanalytic craft, plays a very misleading role, inasmuch as it perpetuates the illusion that the supervisor is much clearer about the patient than the supervisee. There is something oddly infallible about the experience of doing supervision. I don't think this is a consequence of any obvious pecking order in psychoanalytic institutes, but, rather, some odd, seductive aspect of the phenomenology of the supervision process itself. It is extraordinarily out of synchronization with our own clinical experience, and is misleading to our supervisees, inasmuch as they are led to believe that when they "grow up," all will be clear to them, too. It also creates considerable discord in the supervisee's own training analysis, where obviously no such coherence or clarity of concept and purpose can exist.

I believe that this unwarranted clarity is the consequence of what Bateson called (following Bertrand Russell) a "failure in logical typing." That is, a failure to understand that case reports are of an entirely different level of abstraction than therapy.[14] Briefly, the theory of logical typing posits that a class, and the members of the class, are of different levels of abstraction. In other words, a class cannot be a member of itself. Applied to the process of supervision, it follows that what we are doing is discussing a *class* of transactions of which the particular patient is a *member.* We are never really discussing, in supervision, a specific patient, but a class of transactions applicable to *all* patients and illustrated by a specific patient. The apparent clarity is a consequence of this step up in abstraction level. As Count Korzybski noted, the illusion of clarity increases with the level of abstraction.[15] If the supervisor were really to participate in, for example, "parallel process"—that is, to become part of the therapy—he would be largely rendered speechless, since it would become evident that the interactions were so complex that he could say nothing. The moment one moves from the general category of patients for whom this patient is an example to the actual patient, one has plunged into a complex interpersonal morass that is now no longer limited to the treatment room but encompasses all the usual ramifications that proliferate in any analysis. Now there are three participants in a poorly controlled and delimited field. The frame is lost. The number of persons symbolically present increases exponentially and the field becomes virtually chaotic. One is left with a psychoanalysis run wild. Or, what is worse, an occasion for the supervisor to firmly grasp the reins, reestablish order and sequence; and perpetuate, for the hapless candidate, the illusion that psychoanalysis proceeds methodically and according to the canons of hermeneutics.

CHAPTER 12

Harry Stack Sullivan:
The Web and the Spider

The things that everybody wants are
satisfaction and security from anxiety.
—H.S. SULLIVAN

HERETOFORE, I have elaborated a distinction between an intrapsychic psychoanalysis and what I have called, rather loosely, an interpersonal or transactional approach. Harry Stack Sullivan is considered the prime theoretician of the latter position and the gathering point of the great psychoanalytic schism of the 1940s.

As with Freud, it is useful to explore the matrix within which Sullivan's ideas developed, to underscore the chasm of perception that separates these two theorists. Sullivan and Freud represent neither converging nor parallel processes; they reflect different stances entirely. As I suggested in chapter 2, their main point of possible convergence occurred when they both retreated from a path less traveled under the stress of life events. This partial retrenchment, both times accompanied by a revealing dream, drew them to a common point, but not a common path.

It is now over thirty years since Sullivan's death (1949), and there has been much extension and explication of his ideas, and (as is inevitably the case) much radical (back-to-the-roots) reconstruction of his writings. It is often difficult to know exactly where Sullivan was drawing the line in his ideas, partly because he died without pulling his concepts together in a culminating opus and partly because he became, I suspect, diverted and diversified by his embroilment in the bitter Byzantine psychoanalytic politics. Kenneth Chatelaine claims, with supporting opinions, that he did his best work in the relatively pristine milieu of the Washington, D.C.–Baltimore area, prior to his moving to New York in 1930.[1]

Sullivan's interpersonal psychoanalysis seems a theory in transit, still developing and with the implications of many of its postulates left obscure. Sullivan did not, as did Freud, work in heroic isolation.* He was, in a very significant sense, a *conduit* for many other people's ideas. One might claim, with a high degree of paradigmatic consistency, that if Freud was the singular architect of a great psychological edifice, then Sullivan was the processor of an immense amount of information converging from the postwar explosion of information. He was, according to Crowley, an omnivorous reader and autodidact. His avowed background sources read like a library memory bank.

As I contended in *The Fallacy of Understanding*, Freud and Sullivan represent entirely different paradigmatic premises. Thomas Kuhn, in a small but seminal book, *The Nature of Scientific Revolution*, claimed that scientific positions in any era are based on a set of assumptions about the nature of reality, which he called *paradigms*.[3] These paradigms are implicit met-

*Frank Sulloway has claimed in *Freud: Biologist of the Mind* that Freud was not at all as isolated or misunderstood in his work as has been claimed. Freud very much promulgated the myth of the lonely hero, working alone against disapproval and disbelief.[2]

aphors, pervading scientific programs; in the strictest sense, epistemic assumptions. Kuhn was more interested in the phenomenology of change than in the paradigms per se, so he did not specify their individual natures. He did claim that paradigms change discontinuously; that is, they do not gradually shift as the assumptions change, but change rather more consistently with crisis theory, with a buildup of incompatible data, a relatively sudden overload and a new paradigm emerging *with new sponsors.*

The old paradigm lives on with its old coterie of believers, perhaps making surface adjustments to try to assimilate the new model: a version of old wine in new bottles. I said in *The Fallacy of Understanding* that Freud represented an energy machine paradigm and that Sullivan represented an information machine model: the steam engine versus the telephone (or, if one prefers a more technologically-sophisticated version, the jet engine versus the computer). A great deal of confusing overlap is possible. As I suggested, one can make "modern" pronouncements masking an anachronistic paradigm (as do some of the Freudians); one can make modernist statements based on a new paradigm, while giving historical lip-service to the old (as do the object-relationship theorists), or one can present an entirely new paradigm with entirely new premises as an overt statement of rebellion (as did R.D. Laing).[4] Sullivan, I would suggest, did something in between. He presented an entirely fresh perspective based on a communication, or language, paradigm. He quite clearly defined his own participation in new paradigm terms when he openly acknowledged that his theories were an amalgam of many sources of reading and comparison. He had, says Perry, "a growing sense of collective creativity, and an acute awareness of how much one's thoughts and hopes changed dramatically in a new situation with a new person."[5] He read widely, borrowed freely, and preempted sometimes conflicting concepts with only minor modification. He was also sensitive to the ideas of people he had not read, either through hearing them or hearing about them from others. Many of his influences came second- or third-hand. It did not matter, since Sullivan was a control center, a sorter and amalgamator of message. He did not credit, as did Freud (as Perry quotes Freud), "having made a discovery to not being a wide reader. . . . I have denied myself the very great pleasure of reading the works of Nietzsche from a deliberate resolve not to be hampered in working out the impressions received in psycho-analysis by any sort of expectation derived from without."[6]

Freud, like Gilgamesh, makes a lonely journey to the center of the earth to bring back Truth. Sullivan is at the center of a nexus of information extending out to many disciplines and woven, by him, into a coherent web of meaning. I use this web metaphor quite deliberately, since I think that the spider in all his manifestations serves as a unifying trope for many aspects of Sullivan; and it is, very significantly, the central image in the only dream of Sullivan's that we know of in great detail. It will further serve as an armature for a thesis I wish to build around this critical dream of Sullivan's that, as I've indicated, suggests that Sullivan, like Freud, suffered a crisis of intention and backed off from the radical implications of his theory.

Spiders have had a bad psychoanalytic press, the spider being equated with consuming mother.* The unfortunate proclivity of the large female to make a postnuptial lunch of her smaller, presumably trusting, mate lends a certain credence to this view. But the spider is more; it is the maestro of kinesthetics and connection, finely attuned to the world around it. The spider

---

*William Silverberg once had the temerity to suggest the usual psychoanalytic version of the spider to Sullivan; that is, that "spiders generally symbolized the mother." He did it only once.[7]

is his web. It is this exquisite attunement, this sense of connection and relationship, that characterizes Sullivan's position as I shall elaborate it.

To begin with, Sullivan did not proceed from orthodoxy to apostasy, as did Karen Horney, Fromm, and Clara Thompson. He came from an entirely different position, from American Institutional Psychiatry. Sullivan never held a residency in psychiatry, having gone directly to working with ward schizophrenics at St. Elizabeth's under the auspices of William A. White. Not remarkably outstanding at St. Elizabeth's, he went on to Sheppard and Enoch Pratt, a Quaker hospital, where he established a special ward for schizophrenics under Ross McClure Chapman. He became known as a man who spoke the schizophrenic's language and was, from the first, a focus of interest for his skills in reaching heretofore inaccessible, hard-core hospitalized psychotics. His results were considered akin to a miracle.*

Out of his experience with schizophrenics Sullivan elaborated not so much a theory as an extending web of connected percepts taken from psychiatry, anthropology, sociology, biology, ethology: that is, an amalgam of current disciplines. Its power lay in its use of an entirely new paradigm, that of communication and language. Concepts such as empathy, consensual validation, participant-observation, selective inattention (a lateralized concept) are all clearly from a linguistic model. His key concepts of prototaxic, parataxic, and syntaxic are used facilely by therapists who often do not recognize that *taxis* means arrangement and that Sullivan was referring to the ability of the child to *order* experience linguistically. It is through a growing control of language that

*An 8o-percent return to the community was claimed by William Silverberg.[8]

the child is able to invest order into his experience of the world. Much of the development of language, Sullivan felt, occurred through consensual validation—a semantic agreement with another person about the nature of reality. As Chatelaine put it, "It was clear communication that he was after. If a person could clearly articulate and communicate what he is experiencing, he has a grasp on it!"[9]

Presumably, anxiety occurs by contagion. When the parent is anxious, the child becomes anxious. It has been argued that Sullivan thereby defined anxiety as an interpersonal event. Certainly he claimed that the *relief* of anxiety occurs interpersonally and that the self-system develops as a device for avoiding anxiety. Even language, to the extent that it operates as an instrument of the self-system, is used to distance and contain others, to avoid the experience of anxiety.

But what is anxiety? If it is contagiously communicated, then presumably only panicked parents would produce panicked children. Clearly, Sullivan did not believe this to be so; he felt that simple disapproval or withdrawal by a parent could flood a child with anxiety. Surely the child must be demonstrating some readiness for anxiety. As Gerald Chrzanowski has pointed out, Sullivan's theory of anxiety is both central to his thesis and yet its most elusive and contestable element.[10] In Sullivan's words:

> But this concept of anxiety is absolutely fundamental to your understanding what I shall be trying to lay before you. I want to repeat that, because I don't know that I can depend on words really to convey the importance of what I am trying to say: insofar as you grasp the concept of anxiety as I shall be struggling to lay it before you, I believe you will be able to follow, with reasonable success, the rest of the system of psychiatry. Insofar as you presume that I mean *just what you think anxiety is* [emphasis added], I shall have failed to communicate my ideas.[11]

If an anxious parent has defenses, the child is impinged on by the defenses, not the parent's anxiety, unless one postulates an empathic secret in-touchness with something deeply buried in the parent. If anxiety were that telepathic, bypassing semiotic communications, how possibly could a "self-system" protect the child? It would require a lead shield. I think that it is at this point that Sullivan waffles the issue. If it is the experience with the parent that is making the child anxious, then it is because there is something discordant in the experience—say, a mother who makes and breaks eye contact at the wrong frequency, too soon or too late, or fumbles breast feeding. The child then is anxious because something is really wrong and he cannot integrate it. If, on the other hand, the child is responding with panic to the parent's anxiety, regardless of the explicit message, then he has a readiness for anxiety and it is a *drive*, as much as libido or hunger. The child has an incipient terror that is contained, held in check, by the parent's empathic response. Then it is not interpersonal. "Drive" can be defined as:

a genetically determined psychic constituent that, when operative, produces a state of psychic excitement or, as we often say, of tension. This tension impels the individual to activity which is also genetically determined in a general way, but which can be considerably altered by individual experience.[12]

Sullivan's anxiety seems closer to a drive than an interpersonal experience.

It would seem reasonable to wonder why, if Sullivan thought that the organization of experience through language and symbols (a consensually developed and validated skill) was the child's way of controlling his life and avoiding anxiety, he would not believe that anxiety and dread were the manifestations of a breakdown in semiotic control, rather than an intrinsic terror *breaking through* a deficient control system.* It is the same old dichotomy: anxiety as the source of distortion, or anxiety as the consequence of bewildered experience. For Sullivan, the core experience of the child was *incipient* terror caused by a failure of empathy; that is, a feeling of comfort and connection with an unanxious mothering person. If the semiotic controls breaks down, if the child cannot contain his core anxiety, it bursts forth and overwhelms his defenses. The child then distorts his experience. Thus, inadequate defenses lead to anxiety, which leads to distortion, which must be corrected.

Sullivan fell back on the energic model. One might wonder why he defined dynamism as "the relatively enduring pattern of *energy transformations* [emphasis added], which recurrently characterize the organism in its duration as a living organism,"[14] or that:

> The source of the energy of a dynamism lies in the physical needs of the individual. It arises out of his biochemical and biophysical functioning. In its course this energy undergoes various transformations as it produces and travels through emotional reactions and interpersonal relationships. It finds its resolution in some kind of interpersonal event.[15]

Why "energy transformations," when it is clear that informational machines do not exchange energy but *information?*

It sounds very much like Freud's observation of his grandson playing a game, pulling a toy toward him, and then throwing it away, all the time saying, "fort—da!" (here—gone). Freud saw the play as the child's attempts to grapple with the moth-

---

*The former view, that anxiety is a manifestation of a breakdown in the organism's control of its own life, is most clearly expressed by Kurt Goldstein and the existential position as explicated by Rollo May in *The Meaning of Anxiety.*[13]

er's disappearance when she left him.[16] But he saw the language as only a comment on a *fantasy*. The child masters the absence of his mother through fantasying her present, fantasying himself in control of her absence, or wishing her absence vengefully. It took Jacques Lacan's exegesis in linguistic terms to suggest that the child mastered the absence of the mother by putting a *word* in her absence. Where is mother? Not nowhere! *"Gone!"* In the place of the absent mother, a word is substituted and the child is in control. Mother is internalized, inasmuch as in her absence the child has the word. Language is the tool par excellence for binding and mastering experience.[17]

Sullivan's clinical material clearly suggests the same awareness of the function of language. A superficial perusal would lead one to believe that he was using a communication paradigm. But it is not entirely so. Let me repeat (since it is an extremely elusive distinction, from the semiotic view): if the child loses the grasp of his world, if something is going on which he does not understand, conflicting or incoherent messages are received, and anxiety *results.* * The anxiety, from this perspective, is the alarm system. It does not motivate, but is the consequence of, mystification. At the root is a *real* confusion. On the other hand, if one sees the child as in an incipient state of anxiety because this imbalance is his biological nature (a dependency on empathic reassurance) then a breakdown in semiotic control permits the monster in the center to rush forward and consume the child. The anxiety is an energic force, always present, under restraint, and ready to break through defenses. Distortion is the result of untrammeled anxiety. It is wrong and must be corrected: it is not, as in a communicational mode, a distorted message with a real referent. To paraphrase

---

*Increasingly, it is becoming likely that this interactional perception begins very early, perhaps at birth or in utero.

Chrzanowski, anxiety is, for Sullivan, the fire—not, as for Freud, the fire alarm.[18]

It is clear that, for Sullivan, mental disorder results from inadequate interpersonal communication, the communication process *being interfered with by anxiety.*[19] The self-system is itself "an organization of educative experience called into being by the necessity to avoid or to minimize incidents of anxiety."[20] In the beginning, for Sullivan, is not the Word, but inchoate anxiety. Language ameliorates anxiety by giving interpersonal potency, and the self develops as the instrument of social security and competence. The social self does not develop because the potential is there for an emergent social self, but to avoid anxiety. It is a view of humanness as a defense against terror. If there were no cave bears, no saber-toothed tigers, would man not have discovered fire?

It is a pinched and frightened view of human potentials; personality is the accretion of interpersonal operations. There is no individuality; man is the sum of his operations. Peirce, the forerunner of Sullivan's concepts of selfhood, had a more sanguine view. Peirce agreed with John Lincourt's quote of John Greenleaf Whittier: "Man is not primarily a 'symbol-using animal'; rather man is constituted of symbols."[21] Contrary to Lincourt's claim, Sullivan did not agree with that formulation; for, if man is constituted of symbols, he symbolizes because that is his nature, not because he is terrified. For Peirce, the self is a construct for exploring the world, for determining ignorance and error. In sum, the self may be seen as emergent, exploring its own potentials, because it is "there"; or the self may be seen as accretion of defenses against anxiety.

I can recall, as a neurology resident, being astounded by the incoherent rage that would emerge from perfectly amiable aphasic patients if they were asked some simple question they

could not answer. "What is your name?" would convert a
kindly old gentleman into a maniac, kicking over his side table,
throwing his spectacles, and cursing with astonishing depth
and fluency. The same dis-ease, to a lesser degree, can be observed by anyone who has suffered an exasperating lapse of
memory.

I would claim that anxiety is not a *vis a tergo* but a response
to a real danger in the world, which is amplified because the
danger cannot be translated into language concepts. The more
obscure the danger, the greater the anxiety. Sullivan left us a
strange phobic heritage about the nature of anxiety, and we
still tend to treat extreme anxiety as nothing but impending
disaster, better to be ameliorated than faced. Sullivan taught
us that terrifying dreams, ones that awaken the patient and
where the feeling of dread hangs on into the waking day, are
small schizophrenic episodes and should not be analyzed. Indeed, Sullivan had no use for the analysis of dreams as such,
using them only to lead him back to the daytime residues,
which could then be directly dealt with.

> To deal with it on the basis that one can convert dreams or myths
> into consensually valid statements by intellectual operations seems
> to me such a misunderstanding . . . that I don't see how one can
> take it seriously.[22]

Sullivan reports a dream of his own that he uses to illustrate
this theme. He does not think the dream is analyzable, but I
think it illuminates an extraordinary layering of the very issues
I have been exploring.

According to Perry, it was shortly before Sullivan left St.
Elizabeth's Hospital for his new post as an assistant psychiatrist
at Enoch Pratt that he had a dream in which a spider was fea-
tured in a terrifying way.[23] He had the dream:

at the time when it became possible, finally, for me really to start on an intensive study of schizophrenia, partly by my own efforts and largely by accident; and I had decided on this study and all the arrangements were satisfactory. You all recall the geometric designs that spiders weave on grass, and that show up in the country when the dew's on the ground. My dream started with a great series of these beautiful geometric patterns, each strand being very nicely midway between the one in front of it and the one behind it, and so on—quite a remarkable textile, and incidentally, I am noticeably interested in textiles. Then the textile pattern became a tunnel reaching backward after the fashion of the tunnel-web spiders, and then the spider began to approach. And as the spider approached, it grew and grew into truly stupendous and utterly horrendous proportions. And I awakened extremely shaken and was unable to obliterate the spider, which continued to be a dark spot on the sheet which I knew perfectly well would re-expand into the spider if I tried to go to sleep. So instead, I got up and smoked a cigarette and looked out the window and one thing and another, and came back and inspected the sheet, and the spot was gone. So I concluded that it was safe to go back to bed. Now, I'm not going to tell you all about what that meant, because only God knows what I dreamed; I've just told you what I recalled. I'm trying to stress the hang-over, the utter intrusion into sensory perception which required the shaking off of the last vestige of sleep process, the definite reassertion of me and mine, Washington, and what not, in order to prevent the thing from going on. Fortunately, with some assistance, I guessed what might be the case, and thus escaped certain handicaps for the study of schizophrenia. I might add that spiders thereupon disappeared forever from my sleep—so far as I know.[24]

Sullivan distinguished between night terrors, which were devoid of content, and nightmares, which he defined as "dreadful dreams with recollectable content." Although nightmares represented a "grave emergency" in personality, they were at least accessible to recall and offered the possibility of using interpersonal relationships, either to validate the threat in some "curious attempt" or, at least, to reach out to another person to over-come isolation and dread.[25] Perry claims that Sullivan may have gone to William Alanson White for some "assistance," although it is not clear what this "parting gift" could possibly have been, considering Sullivan's unenthusiastic pronouncements about the therapeutic use of dreams.[26]

Sullivan revealed that, when he was between the ages of two-and-a-half and four, a dead spider was put at the top of the stairs to "discourage my ambulatory efforts" which, we are told in seeming justification, had often resulted in his falling down the stairs. He sneeringly refers to the psychoanalytic cli-ché, "if one considers that the spider is a mother symbol . . . one can picture what profound problems I had in repressing my hostility to the mother, or something of the sort. But I pre-fer to say, simply, that I didn't like spiders, and I disliked them so much that I wouldn't pass one . . ."[27]

Notice that "someone" put a dead spider on the stairs to "discourage my ambulatory efforts." Why did not Sullivan re-port that it was, according to Perry, his grandmother who per-petrated this bizarre bit of restraint when he was a child?[28] The event occurred during a year's period when he was living with his grandmother, his mother having mysteriously disap-peared. She was rumored to have had a psychotic breakdown, but there appears to be no firm evidence of this—only that when she returned she seemed "changed." Sullivan ignores the real experience and mockingly makes reference to the Freudian saw, spider equals mother. "But I prefer to say, simply, that I don't like spiders." Why so simply? His relationship with his mother was very complex. She had married late (at age thir-ty-nine), and was several years older than her husband, whose social status was well beneath her family's expectations. Harry was her only child, two previous sons having each died at under a year of age. She spent much time with him and filled his imagination with her tales of the aristocratic Stacks and their adventures.

Notice that he is fascinated by the pattern of the web, which he equates with his "interest in textiles." Note that the root of textile is the Latin *textus,* or woven thing. At the center of the beautiful textual or contextual organization resides the spider, Sullivan's center of terror, which leaps forth to devour the unwary. At the center of organization and order lives chaos.

Even the most lustrous metapsychology has at its core, like the grain of sand that provokes the formation of the pearl, a particle of personal psychopathology. For Sullivan, all semiotic skills are developed to contain the terror at the center of things. That terror, for Sullivan, is inchoate, before language, even before experience, except of the most primitive empathic nature. But this thesis makes it possible for Sullivan to "inattend" that someone using a phobic object to deter his explorations was a lunatic piece of malevolence, that the dream occurs as he is about to "extend" his "ambulatory efforts," to move to another institution and begin a radical new approach to schizophrenia. Sullivan implies that the move to study schizophrenics activates his own schizophrenic core, *not* that he is terrified that his ambulatory efforts to grow and learn and enrich himself may be blocked in some way he will have trouble comprehending and dealing with—which is exactly what happened. Sullivan lost his ward, in spite of efforts on the part of the hospital director, Ross McClure Chapman, to support him. He left in 1930 to come to New York, where he became embroiled in the politics of American psychoanalysis.

I am suggesting that the dream is not only accessible but vitally *usable.* Structurally, it presents the dialectic between organization and chaos. It is a dream precipitated by a move. It is terrifying to Sullivan because he cannot identify what had been done to him originally and in what way that is being recapitulated. His relationships with both White at St. Elizabeth and Chapman at Sheppard and Enoch Pratt are extremely obscure and ambiguous. Sullivan only worked under White for eight months. Ross McClure Chapman took on Sullivan at Sheppard and Enoch Pratt on the basis of a rather ambivalent and lackluster letter of recommendation from White: "I really did not know Dr. Sullivan very well. (He manifested) . . . discontent that might express itself in alliance with other discontented spirits."[29] Chapman, in contrast, strongly championed the young Sullivan and his audacious views of the treatment of psychotics. Chatelaine reports being told repeatedly that "if there had been no Chapman, there would have been no Sullivan."[30] Yet, in spite of the unusual relationship of closeness and respect between Chapman and Sullivan, Sullivan was forced to leave Sheppard after seven years ostensibly because of his financial insouciance. There was, however, a considerable hue and cry about his special ward for young male schizophrenics and its rumored homosexual ambience.

On a profounder structural level, Sullivan's dream represents his theoretical posture—that he is fascinated by organization and networks, but he sees at the core of it something else, an ineffable horror. Webs entangle only the unwary. Sullivan's interest in detailed inquiry, precise perceptions, consensual validation—all the concepts that belong properly to a communication model—were attributed secondary roles as "defenses against" something else, an energic center. Sullivan's theory is, in the end, as phobic as his fear of spiders. Why not look closely and discredit the danger? I suspect that a combination of his own psychodynamics, which predicated against "seeing" as much as did Freud's, potentiated by his embroilment in a dislocated, essentially European psychoanalytic movement, led him to stop short of the full implications of his position. The language and conceptualizations of Sullivan are so clearly in a semiotic model, however, that they have served comfortably as bridges to the next paradigm for the next generation of interpersonal psychoanalysts.*

If Freud identified himself with Oedipus, of whom Tiresias, the blind seer, sneeringly said, when Oedipus was being blindest, "It is in riddle answering you are strongest," then Sullivan is the Tiresias of the myth.[32] Tiresias was, as was Sullivan, a man of very obscure background. It was said that he had died and been revived; that he had been turned into a woman for watching two snakes couple; that he had been struck blind for watching Athena bathe, or for not deciding favorably in a dispute between the gods; that he was given the gift of prophesy by Zeus, who felt sorry for him—hardly a blessing, since it guaranteed him virtual social ostracism. Sullivan, too, was isolated, mysterious, inconsistent, somewhat disreputable, somewhat epicene; a man who had (he, himself—rumored but never confirmed) journeyed to the underground (had had a schizophrenic experience). Tiresias' foresight lay in his nexus of experience. He had traveled every arm of the crossroads, experienced every paradox; was portentous, but hardly heroic.

---

*Concepts of participant-observation or consensual validation have been extended far past the limited usage of Sullivan. See Laurence Epstein and Arthur Feiner's *Countertransference* for elaboration.[31]

CHAPTER 13

Object-Relations Theory:

Bridge or Bypass

Most dreadful are its divinities, most
feared, Daughters of darkness
and mysterious earth.
                    —*Oedipus at Colonus*

ONE CAN in a relatively straightforward fashion define the difference between traditional Freudian drive theory and interpersonal theory, but it has been argued that this divisiveness is more historical than real. Object-relations theory, it is claimed, has provided a bridge between these heretofore incompatible positions. All object-relations theories offer some contention that real persons in the child's surrounding matter and that early mother-child relationships, long antedating language and the triangulated family, predestine the child's developmental outcome.

These theories do not cluster around the conflict issues of the Oedipus triangle but around the mysteries of *mütterrecht;* not the phallic father but the early terrible mother goddess. It is of some interest that the progenitor of these theories was a woman, Melanie Klein, and that their most extensive acceptance, until recently, was in England, a country with a long history of matriarchal leadership.

In a loose continuum of positions, ranging from Klein through W. Ronald Fairbairn, Harry Guntrip, Winnicott, John Bowlby, and Bion, these theorists dissociate themselves from libido theory and conceptualize drive as "object-seeking"; that is, the child's primary drive is to make contact with the primal mother, the source of all life. Even Melanie Klein, whose theory is most instinctually based, wherein "perceptions of real objects are merely the scaffolding for projections of the child's innate object images," postulates that real experience with real mothering ameliorates the destructive "phantasy" systems.[1]

The political consequences of this adaptation of classical theory can be well imagined, ranging from denunciations of heresy to ecumenical calls to unification. Kernberg, the self-defined American representative of object-relations theory, shuttles between Avignon and Rome, to the exasperation of some Freudians, who consider him an apostate, and to the relief of others, who hail him as the great bridgemaker of contemporary psychoanalysis.[2] To be sure, not the slightest attention is paid to the somewhat parallel efforts of Sullivan and the interpersonalists, although Sullivan's concepts of the interpersonal field, "good-me, bad-me" personifications and "empathy," would seem to be sympathetic to the object-relations concepts, particularly those of Fairbairn.[3] Sullivan's position, as I've suggested, is enigmatic. To the extent that he shares a drive paradigm, there is much similarity; but there are also significant differences inherent in Sullivan's open-ended use of interpersonal process.

Object-relations theory is firmly imbedded in a drive concept; the nature of the drive is changed from libido to object seeking. In this sense, a drive is defined, at least by implication, as any inherent, sustained, powerful impulse in the infant and child; libido, need for the breast, for human contact, even Sullivan's "anxiety." The drive must be contained, defenses are set up, and the drive emerges in distorted form. The defenses are never entirely adequate to the job of containment and the infant is consequently warped by the experience. The more powerful the drive, the earlier, developmentally, are its manifestations. In object-relations theory the person's most important and determining experience is early mother-child bonding, before the development of language. Inherent is the presumed primitive nature of infantile thought, consistent with the model of topological suppression, wherein the deeper layers of experience (that is, the earliest) are most primitive and most requiring of sophisticated control. The infant's fantasies constitute a virtual nursery Krafft-Ebing. They are fragmented, sadistic, depressed, and bizarre. Childhood is spent integrating these crude and partial percepts into a workable image of the world.

The impact of real experience is disputed, ranging from Klein's claim that the distortions are drive-motivated to the perceptions of Fairbairn and Winnicott that they reflect real experience with less than adequate mothering. Nevertheless, certain consistent assumptions remain: first, that the critical development period is very early mother-child bonding; second, that the child encapsulates primitive, infantile perceptions of others which remain into adulthood and which, demonically, control his adult relationships. To quote Jay Kwawer, "For all object-relations theories, neurosis is an organized pattern of dealings with a primitive or psychotic or dissociated or schizoid core of universal experience."[4] Consequently, therapy becomes an exorcism. Infancy is not the beginning of a lifetime of accumulating symbolic experience with others; it is a basic flaw. It is a grim Victorian perspective; one must struggle all one's life with nursery injuries, the failure to have a good enough mother or to be a good enough child.

To the extent that Sullivan promulgated his position that the self developed to avoid anxiety, that disturbances in mother-child empathy resulted in a release of anxiety, and that the child would do anything to avoid anxiety, one might reasonably claim that Sullivan's position is compatible with object-relations theory. Yet, Sullivan's clinical work suggests a semiotic paradigm. It is not that the child has good experiences which cure him of his early fantasies but that he develops the semiotic skills to proceed from a prototaxic to a parataxic to a syntaxic arranging of reality. That is, the child learns through language to order experience in some manageable and mutually validatable fashion. He masters and *binds* experience through language; he does not convalesce from an infantile psychosis through a corrective emotional experience or a controlled regression. Sullivan's child matures by understanding through language what is happening in his world.

Even "empathy," which Sullivan considered to be some ineffable communication between mother and infant, is now clearly observable in the form of semiotic exchanges between mother and child, almost from birth. The rhythms of eye contact, suckling, and breathing are interactional. Rather than an epigenetic sequence in which the person proceeds linearly from stage to stage unless interrupted and "fixated," one has a more holistic vision of the person actively developing an increasingly complex fabric of relationship, expanding and sophisticating his connection to the world. From this viewpoint, the adult is not stuck with an incorporated infant, like a fishbone in the craw of his maturity; rather, he or she is having much the same experience at twenty years as at twenty months, except on a more semiotically complex level. The mother who cannot handle breast feeding because the infant "bites" is the same mother who tells the child that she had to stop breast feeding "because you bit me so hard I got sore" is the same mother who withdraws her support from the preadolescent who talks back, is the same mother at eighty who complains to her grandchildren that her daughter doesn't "let her help." Parenting has a fearsome symmetry. The child learns his language from his parents and speaks with their accent. He perpetuates the network of warped relationships because he becomes what he beholds and because he proceeds to create a continuous milieu. The present patient is disabled by a present semiotic defect, not by an encapsulated infantile or childhood set of experiences.

How does the patient "get better?" The object-relations model depends heavily on regression in the transference and interpretation. Controlled regression may require, as in Winnicott, an active holding on the part of the therapist, but the infantile fantasies must be engaged. Then how does the therapist, whose instrument is speech, talk to a prelanguage fantasy? The consequence is, at least to the uninitiated, a bizarre reversion to the *malleus maleficarum,* in which the therapist evokes the demon within. *Vide* James Grotstein: "She especially feels that her mother was very upset with her from the first time she had sex. I interpreted that she feels that she has stolen her mother's sex and left her menopausal and bleeding and now has her installed inside of her as a useless impediment and also as a guilt-producing reminder (combination of obstructive and albatross objects)."[5]

Granted that this is quoted out of context; still, to whom or what inside the patient is the therapist talking? Who understands this interpretation? The patient's healthy ego in alliance with the therapist? How does *it* get the message across to the infantile residues? Perhaps it is more important to know what the patient's experiences with her mother have been around the issues of sexuality, competition, and envy. Is this patient ill because she has distorted her perception of her relationship with her mother or does she have an accurate perception of a distorted relationship? The implications of this distinction are immense.

It leads to an entirely different view of transference. As reported in an article by Meltzer, a young man comes to treatment because of repeated failures in relationships and in school.[6] His pattern is characterized by a premonitory success and then a collapse. He begins therapy, improves rapidly, and then predictably hits the doldrums. A reality event precipitates a long dream that is brilliantly interpreted by Meltzer as a birth trauma dream. The next session, the patient tells of another dream, in which he has been ordered to behead a little boy. He proceeds with the task in a listless, alienated way. The little boy develops some strength and begins to resist. The weapon used is a scimitar, which led, by association, to the therapist's car. The therapist is represented as a Negro, which "puzzles" him. The dream is seen as an excellent illustration of the mechanism of splitting. But the simpler observation—that the patient sees himself in another situation, in which he is going to cut off his own head, where he will be subject to another person's ambitions for him and to the expectation that he understand and change; that he has characteristically, after an initial cooperation, listlessly submitted to his own death—does not get taken up. Perhaps the real issue is the therapist's ambitions and expectations for this patient and the patient's experience that no one is really interested in what he feels or thinks. He is a battlefield for others' wars. He came into treatment because he had failed entrance to Oxford. Whose ambition was that?

Rather than seeing the relationship with the patient as a real mutual encounter that must be examined in meticulous detail, the therapist evokes his demons. Drive predicates defense. Defense predicates distortion. Distortion predicates anachronism; the infant lives on in the adult in a time warp. The transference is not two adults talking to each other about their private agendas and expectations but one adult, the therapist, talking to the demonic infant within the patient.

CHAPTER 14

Conclusion

It remains for the future to decide
whether there is more delirium in my
theory than I should like to admit or
whether there is more truth in
Schreber's delusions than other people
are prepared to believe.

—S. FREUD

THERE IS a Zen saying that the last thing you learn is the first. I must end by asking the question I started with. Who dreams the dream? Does the dream perhaps dream the dreamer? Freud's reference to the Schreber case is an exemplary instance of the razor's edge on which the issue of psychological reality rests. Schreber's paranoid delusions have been documented point by point by Schatzman as transformations of Schreber's actual experience with his father.[1] Schatzman has made a telling case for the reality of Schreber's experience. Still, Schreber was clearly psychotic.

Was Schreber mad because of his experience with his father? Or did Schreber fashion out of his own unconscious pressures a psychotic representation of a relationship with his father, which, albeit bizarre to our eyes, was not so uncommon for the times? Although Schreber's father was a highly regarded pedagogue, and his books were taken seriously, hardly considered sadistic meanderings, still Daniel Gustave, Schreber's brother, also became psychotic and committed suicide. At least one of three sisters suffered severe emotional problems. The case for D.P. Schreber's distortion of a normal family seems strained unless one postulates a hereditary diathesis.

It is here, presumably, that the road bifurcates: the intrapsychic position requires that the patient confront the gap between reality and fantasy—the interpersonal position that he see that it is people who damage people and that, if the enormity of his experience at his father's hands can be conceptualized, put into language, he will be released.

This is no simple issue; both positions lend themselves to oversimplification. If, as the case material presented in chapter 8 suggests, an analyst can play at being a Pope, then an interpersonalist can, with equal self-indulgence, play at being a missionary. Psychoanalysis Saves! Resolving mystifications cannot simply be showing the patient how abused and misled he has been. I suspect that R.D. Laing's praxis foundered on this point. He was telling in his presentation of the process of mystification, but far less convincing about how to demystify. How was the patient to change? Out of gratitude for the therapist's support? As an abreaction of dissociated rage?

People resist change. This is axiomatic in every system of psychotherapy of any subtlety. Showing the way, corrective emotional experience, abreaction of feeling all help, but it is only when the patient's investment and participation in the very system that mystifies him is actualized that change becomes possible. To explain this apparent intransigence, the intrapsychic therapist postulates mechanism; the interpersonalist and some of the object-relations therapists postulate a self-system, about which Sullivan said, "Anything which would seriously disturb the equilibrium, any event which tends to bring about a basic change in an *established pattern* of dealing with others, sets up the tension of anxiety and calls for activities for its relief."[2] It is what made an energic postulate so appealing to both Freud and Sullivan: the therapist, attempting to open the door for the patient, gets a very strong sense that someone is leaning in from the other side, a resisting *force*.

But it is not necessary to posit "resistance." A more parsimonious extension of the concept of participant-observation would lead one to observe that the therapist has no real leverage for change because he is grounded in the same phenomenal field as the patient. To lift the patient, he must lift himself. Dare one say that the patient does not change *because change is not being offered* but, rather, a more extensive, laterally extending participation in the same system? And, that the reason the therapist is part of the field he is trying to shift lies in the nature of the psychoanalytic algorithm, as I outlined it?

It is odd that Sullivan wavered on locating the self-system. If the self is in dynamic equilibrium, maintained by the patient's "dynamisms" *and* by reflected appraisals, then it is truly in the interpersonal field. The self is maintained by the people who make up the subject's world. If I was bad because Mommy thought I was bad, then I *am* bad because I not only act bad but because others expect me to act bad, need my badness, inattend my efforts not to be bad, and, moreover, I select them for that, elicit that response from them. If I work with a therapist, he will start by assuring me that I am not bad, but in the fullness of the analysis, he will come to treat me just as the others have.

Sullivan said,

The psychiatrist will often discover that the patient is living by standards which were inculcated in childhood, *but which he knows from other experiences are not valid* [emphasis added]. But since the patient can't formulate what he knows, he goes on in the same old way.[3]

If the patient does not know what he knows, what stops him from knowing? A "dynamism" is postulated.

I would disagree. First, if he cannot formulate it, he doesn't know it. From my perspective, knowing, indeed being, is coterminous with language. Very likely the patient does not "know" that his way of life is invalid; he may not like it, but he knows it works. It is *very* valid, if limiting in possibilities. To surrender it for an ambiguity with which he cannot deal would be far worse. A paranoid knows that believing everyone is untrustworthy is not a very happy way of life and requisitions a great deal of loneliness that other people seem to avoid. But he doesn't know how they manage to do it! When he tries to be accessible, he misreads the signs, fails to hit the right note, offends people by getting too close or standing off too far. His rhetoric is faulty, his proxemics are poor, everything goes wrong. So he goes back to what is valid for him—the redundant assumption that everyone is out to get him. The consequences are predictable and safe. He stays clear, and so do they. He avoids more serious trouble.

But perhaps he acts this way not because a dynamism insists but because he doesn't know a better way of performing. A patient washing up in the company bathroom is jokingly told by a companion that he splashes water on himself like a seal. He responds, laughingly, "And you look like a horse!" The other person is offended, and he is bewildered. Is it his deep-seated rage emerging, or has he not mastered the rhetoric of playful insult? One stops looking like a seal when one stops splashing. To look like a horse is a lifetime investiture in big teeth and offset ears. It is like Samuel Johnson's retort to a famously ugly woman who told him that he stank. "Yes, Madame," he said, "but *I* can always bathe." The paranoid learns that it is safer to stay aloof and humorless and, thus, avoid a serious contretemps.

One can see much the same confusion of levels in Gregory Bateson's material.[4] Bateson, the father of the double-bind theory of schizophrenia, could hardly be considered naïve about levels, yet consider the following material: Bateson, visiting the home of a schizophrenic patient, is impressed with the sterility and neatness of the home. He decides to buy some gladioli, since they are both "beautiful and untidy," as he tells the mother, presenting her with the flowers. "Oh!" she said, "Those are not untidy flowers. As each one withers, you can snip it off." Bateson notes, with wry amusement, the castrative message, but he is more interested in what he sees as the mother's psychopathology. Bateson sees the mother as *doing* something to her son, malevolently and with intent driving him crazy. Why not think that the mother simply missed his irony; or that his irony was inappropriate, that he was grandstanding for the patient, who was standing by through this exchange?

Consider an alternative scenario: Bateson presents her with the flowers and his speech. She says, "Untidy? Why untidy? Are you suggesting, Dr. Bateson, that you think my housekeeping is obsessional and my home sterile?" What would Bateson then say? "Yes, that's what I had in mind."? It would be evident that it was a grandstand play to the observing patient, that Bateson was *counting on* her responding inappropriately. Were she not to, he would stand revealed in a piece of extreme gaucherie. One notes that gladiolus is from the diminutive of the Latin for sword. Was Bateson perhaps beating his sword into flowers, not ploughshares? He must attribute malevolence to the mother, make her his "schizophrenogenic mother," because, without anxiety, he has no energic push to justify the son's defense of insanity.

Perhaps Bateson's best-known example of the double-bind is the young man, "fairly well recovered" from an acute schizophrenic episode, visited by his mother in the hospital. "He was glad to see her and impulsively put his arms around her shoulders." (How is Bateson so sure of the patient's feelings?) Whereupon she stiffens. The son retreats, and his mother asks, "Don't you love me anymore?" He blushes, and she says that he shouldn't be so shy and afraid of his feelings. For Bateson, the double message is clear. If you love, I rebuff you; if you feel rebuffed, I tell you you shouldn't fear loving feelings. The patient is demolished by what Bateson calls the mother's "masterful" condemnation.[5]

But Bateson excludes himself from his own frame. After all, he was there, watching all this; he was part of it. Surely the patient had discussed his mother with some therapist at the hospital. Why would he expect her to respond to a warm gesture when they had had trouble touching each other for a lifetime? Or, did he expect her to respond? Was he perhaps showing off for the therapist? Or setting her up? Had someone convinced him that if he were warm and loving his mother would respond? Is his sense of timing seriously off? Was the mother lamely trying to recover from what she now saw as a gaffe? It is not so simple.

Bateson says that the schizophrenic syndromata are "related to an inability to know what sort of a message a message is."[6] For Bateson, the patient's problem is that he cannot identify the hostility or destructiveness in what the mother is doing. Supposing one said, instead, that the difficulty is the inability to stay with the helically-expanding layering of message upon message that includes his therapists, the hospital, Bateson, and the funding organization that supported Bateson's research, let alone his family with all its enmeshments. A less disabled patient might think, "Why the devil did I reach out like that? What did I really think would happen? Maybe she's afraid of me. Would I have done it if Dr. Bateson were not watching?" After all, didn't Bateson try to "mousetrap" the mother, in the previous example, with flowers?

I am in perfect agreement with the idea that some form of semiotic confusion *is* the problem. It seems far less clear whether the "mystification" of "double-binding" comes about out of anxiety, as Freud, Sullivan, and Bateson suggest, or whether it is a family defect, passed on from generation to generation, difficult for the person to identify, since it is an omission of experience, rather than an act, a commission. These semiotic defects may be like visual scotomata. A person unaware that there is a gap in vision may react nonetheless with uneasiness, fearfulness, and irritability. It is conceivable that certain semiotic blind spots may be genetic, passed through a family like dyslexia or difficulty with mathematics. It may be that to some extent they are not defects per se but genetic cognitive differences that become maladaptive when they run up against a social situation requiring the absent skill. It may be (and we hope it is) that they are socially learned in the family subculture. It is the old psychoanalytic debate about regression/fixation. Is the patient stuck at a certain developmental level, or does he, under the stress of drives, retreat to an earlier level of development? The answer is not yet in. One hopes for a range of flexibility in patients. Some patients can utilize latent skills developed in the course of therapy. Other patients may learn by rote or imitation how to get by but never really "play the game."

These latter patients can be educated in a more sophisticated mode of relating. There are versions of psychodrama and group therapy which do just that. Without the validating working through of experience with the therapist, however, this remains merely an accomplished "as if" performance. Some people do get to be very good at it, often by a deliberate preadolescent or adolescent act of will, and it is difficult to ascertain, under their personae of competence, their extreme vulnerability.

If Schreber was driven crazy by his father, he remains crazy because it becomes a calling. He is not equipped to be anything else. Schreber's delusions were, in Freud's words, "truth," but delusions nonetheless, because he could not find a pragmatic base for believing that what his father was doing to him was wrong. His feelings had no consensual validation. Since his father doubtless believed he was doing the right thing, there would be a very powerful reinforcing feedback about the normalcy of his experience.* If a therapist were to tell Schreber that his father's behavior was malevolent, Schreber would not believe him. Why should he? The therapist might have his own motives for making trouble. Maybe *he* needed straightening out, a stint in one of Schreber père's corsets. Or, even if the therapist is right, Schreber must take it on faith, which puts him right back into a totally untenable state of dependency. It may be that if in time and after long testing he learns to trust the therapist, *and* on that ground changes his behavior with others, *and* has reinforcing positive experiences, change will occur. But it is still reform. At the first breakdown of the network of support, he will revert to what he knows best and what works best—namely, offending and alienating people.

What Sullivan called the self-system is nothing more than a mechanism for producing redundancy, that is, eliciting predictable, replicable responses from the world. In his famous paper "On the Illusion of Personal Individuality" Sullivan reiterated his "We are all more simply human than otherwise" dictum.[8] He claimed that as far as he could see there was no such thing as genuine uniqueness of personality: that there are as many personalities as there are fields of interaction. Making a case for the operational interpersonal nature of psychoanaly-

---

*Schreber's father said, "All your dealings with the child, all your influences upon it must be founded on love, i.e., on true, pure and sensible love."[7]

sis, he could have, as well, simply said that the uniqueness of personality was not subject to psychoanalytic inquiry. Indeed, it has been claimed subsequently that this was his position. However, as Clara Thompson pointed out and as a reading of Sullivan will attest, his position was much more radical than that.[9] It seems like a rather odd thesis for so utterly eccentric and idiosyncratic a man.[10] But, surely, children are not just panic-stricken and learning how to cope. They are also intriguing, unique people who are not simply avoiding anxiety, or even solving problems, but exercising inherent potentials for growth. Relatedness, in the informational model, is a biosocial given, an a priori.

Anyone who has seen an infant grab his crib bars, pull himself to his feet, and, unable to sit down, stand there weeping until he is lowered by the parent, and then, instantly, beaming with power, hoist himself up again for an interminable (at least, to the parent) repetition of this play cannot believe that the self is developed to avoid anxiety. Why wouldn't the child stay put?

It is known from Noam Chomsky's work on generative-transformational grammar that the child has an inherent prestructured sense of language.[11] He learns language because the rules are built in and held common to all languages. It is equally likely that, in addition to semantics and syntax, there is a built-in potential for understanding and ordering the pragmatics of communication. In a word, children learn because they have the potential to learn. There is a universe of subtle message that the child must master to be potent in the world. Sullivan implies that, under the stress of anxiety, an aspect of the self, the self-system, operates to concretize, disregard, and constrict experience until the person feels safe. If that mechanism fails, anxiety stampedes the defenses and a schizophrenic panic results.

It is also possible, as I suggested earlier, that for a variety of reasons the person has not learned the intricate grammar of interpersonal relationships. By the time he enters the preadolescent world, his accent, so to speak, is so bad that others shun him. Thus, impotence may be a consequence of impotent experience, not necessarily a defense against anxiety. When the patient is exposed to others, including the therapist, he panics if he goes in over his head, does not understand what is happening, cannot conceptualize it.

It is a sobering experience for a therapist to treat a patient individually and in a group and to hear the patient tell the group what you, the analyst, said to him earlier in the day. Sometimes, it is barely recognizable. Is this because of the patient's anxiety, or because there is a semiotic gap? I am not suggesting that anxiety does not play an important role, but I am questioning the drive-therapy assumption that it motivates behavior.

In working with adolescents, it is common to hear about the controlling, demanding, nagging mother who is always after her child to clean up his or her room, comb his or her hair. If one asks whether anyone ever *does* what the mother demands, one learns that, surprisingly, she is largely ignored and treated with disdain by children and husband. She is an ogre—in intent, not effect. They are all passively-aggressively resisting her. There is a great deal of rage, helplessness, and unresolved dependency in the air. It's an old psychoanalytic aphorism that your patient's mother is someone else's patient. When the mother becomes the nominal patient, the therapist can then see *her* as victimized by her family and their needs.

Suppose, instead of saying that this family is "needy" or "hostile" or "passive-aggressive" or "seductively overinvolved," one suggested that they are not able to sustain relationships with one another, to be competent to show need, detach when they have had enough, utilize each other in a competent way. It begins to sound like the "borderline" family—unable to define and sustain interpersonal boundaries. But one can see the same mechanism in hysterical families.

If it is true that paranoids have trouble reading metamessages, nuances of communication, then hysterics simply do not believe that people mean what they say. I recall a young man of fourteen whose mother would pull on his socks and tie his shoes every morning as he lay in bed. He would protest volubly; she would rage at him for subjecting her to this service. Neither one believed a word the other was saying. One day, he said quietly to her, "Mother, I'm old enough to do that for myself." She looked up at him in amazement and never did it again—with real relief, I might add. How could it change so suddenly, if "needs" alone are involved?

A young woman with a great deal of somaticized depression denies endlessly, to her therapist, that she feels sad. As she crosses the street after leaving a session, a hard-hat yells to her, "Hey Honey, cheer up!" She is suddenly aware of her sadness and begins to cry. If one says to a patient, "Your mother sounds like a very hostile and depriving woman," the patient nods agreement. If one says, "Your mother sounds like a real bitch," the very same patient is shocked and leaps to his or her mother's defense. Clearly, insight depends not entirely on content but on semiotics—the timing, the wording, the setting, the rhetoric of the message.

I would suggest, along with Sullivan, that the theorist functions as an expert, but in the semiotics of interpersonal relationships. The therapy functions as a playground for the exploration of semiotic meaning and the learning of semiotic distinctions. The layering upon layer of meaning in the artificially constructed analytic situation makes it a unique opportunity for such inquiry. The antinomies of drive theory disappear, and rather than transference/countertransference one has the therapist as a participant, along with another participant, the patient, in a field they both observe. Participant-observation should not be delegated to the therapist: it is a mutual effort. Catching the therapist in a self-serving operation may do more for the patient's sense of competence than a lifetime of benevolent participations. A therapist who can engage the patient and expect a certain degree of reciprocity and response, or who refuses to work with an uncommitted patient, may do more to advance the therapy than a benumbed, silent psychoanalyst, ensconced behind the couch.

What sustains emotional disturbance? Libido? Anxiety? Both are drive theories. Both require the energy of a dynamism. Both seem to me to be traveling the self-same road. The other path at the crossroads suggests that emotional disturbance is a failure of semiotic competence; that is, a failure in a linguistically-defined and -validated world to develop the necessary skills to identify levels of communication and to call out in others appropriate and useful responses. To be neurotic is to play "Three Blind Mice" on a veritable Stradivarius of semiotic sensitivity. One road suggests that anxiety causes a "tin ear"; the other suggests that a "tin ear" causes anxiety. The difference is not trivial. It evokes an entire shift in paradigm, from a mechanical to an informational model. As I hope the clinical material has illustrated, it evokes a shift from sincerity to authenticity, from insight to enrichment, from clarity and linearity to paradox and circularity.

It also evokes an entirely different attitude about anxiety. Anxiety is no longer the force behind the defenses but, more simply, a response to helplessness. No longer fear of the knife that castrates, or the spider at the center of things, it is merely an index of helplessness. Anxiety is not the enemy. As Dostoyevsky said in *Notes from Underground:*

There's no disputing that man likes creating and building roads. But why does he also like chaos and disorder, even into his old age? Explain that, if you can! . . . And what makes you so cocksure, so positive that only the normal and the positive, that is, only what promotes man's welfare, is to his advantage?[12]

Any jogger, skier, writer, or artist would concur. The assumption is the ordinary social one: anxiety will decrease when the person is competent. A child who sees devils behind every tree is distorting, but he is also lost in the forest, at night.

This view of anxiety is the existential one. Rollo May, in his excellent book *The Meaning of Anxiety,* makes a strong case for viewing anxiety not as a disabling symptom but as the propelling force behind the drive for self-actualization.[13] Anxiety is the state of man when he confronts his potential freedom, said Kierkegaard. But, still, a drive—self-realization—is postulated. Some force (intrapsychic defenses, interpersonal field) must block it, and distortion results. The traditional paradigm of mechanical force remains in effect.

May used an extended clinical example to make his point: the case of "Harold Brown," a disturbed young man who suffered severe anxiety attacks. Two salient memories are presented: first, at age five, his mother had "offered him her breast" while breast feeding his baby sister, with the remark, "Do you want a drink, too?" He felt intensely humiliated "at this implication that he was still a young baby."[14] Second, when he was eight, his mother had "punished him by making him whip her." According to May, "He was dominated by his mother under the formula, 'If you go against my authority, you do not love me.' " The case presentation is a sensitive and perceptive one. But the malevolence of the mother, her *intent* to be damaging, is assumed without question: "If he tries to use his power, to produce and achieve independently of his mother,

he will be killed."[15] The thesis is that the patient's drive to
self-realization is blocked by the mother's destructiveness. Like
a tree pushing up through concrete, Harold Brown is distorted
and dwarfed by the conflict. This seems inarguable. But the
postulated sequence is drive (self-realization), threat (his mother's claim on him), defense (anxious restriction of possibility).
The paradigm remains unchanged.

There is a great temptation, from this perspective, to fall
heir to Alfred North Whitehead's "fallacy of misplaced con-
creteness." The parent (in May's case, the mother) is reified
as a cluster of psychodynamics, not as a person, and the nuances of semiotic exchange are lost. How is it that the mother
behaved that way? If she correctly read his envy and teasingly
or sarcastically offered a breast, it would certainly be humiliat-
ing to the little boy. But, remember, this was the mother who
had him *whip her* to punish him! One suspects that she would
really have given him her breast if he asked. The line between
irony, sarcasm, teasing, and acting-out is decidedly blurred.
The therapist can say accurately that the mother was "a dominating sadomasochistic mother, who exercised her tyranny at
one moment by an assumption of strength, but at other times
by the more effective (and, for Harold) more confusing strategy
of cloaking the tyranny under a pretense of her weakness."[16]
But this attributes to the mother a great deal more intentionality and power than I suspect she really possessed.

Supposing one were to say that the problem Harold is having
with his mother is that she is crazy. One notes the startled reaction: one is not supposed to talk that way about patients and
their families. But, at least, this latter position implies that the
mother is inadequate and that Harold is having troubles not
because his way is blocked by a supernally powerful person but
because his mother is drastically defective in her style of relating. I suspect Harold already knows that; it may be the basis

of his solicitude toward her. Rollo May quotes Goldstein as say-ing, "Does not anxiety constitute intrinsically of that inability to know from whence the danger threatens?"[17] I would claim that the "whence" is not the mother per se but the mother's confusion of levels of message, which is extremely pathological but difficult to catch. It is rather like watching two intermeshed cogwheels turning. One has a tooth missing, and every so often the smooth movement is interrupted by a little skip. A blink of one's eye, and it is missed. I would postulate that his mother, breast feeding her baby, quite accurately identified his envy but *could not respond appropriately.* Something went awry in her response to him, and I do not believe that she intended to be damaging. Another parent would have ignored it, distracted him, offered him a compensatory gratification, even teased him and gotten away with it. I suspect he retains the incident as a marker memory not because he was humiliated (little chil-dren are humiliated a great deal) but because something was "wrong" with the exchange—a "skip" in the smooth gearing of social interaction.

Watch the face of a young child being teased. His relief as he is reassured by the teaser—"this is teasing, *it is not really going to happen"*—is evident. What, then, is the experience of a child who lives in a world where one level of communica-tion melds into another, where metaphor turns into reality? Lots of children have heard the old parental saw "This is going to hurt me a lot more than it hurts you." They also know it's not true. But what of poor Harold, whose mother really does reverse roles, has him whip her to punish him? It is very easy for therapists to deal with concrete content and miss the levels of message. Harold's presenting symptom was examination anxiety, and to take examinations successfully is to "know" the answer. This man knows that, in some profoundly unrealized way, something strange is going on.

To learn that his mother is hostile or overprotective simply perpetuates the myth of his mother's power. To learn that, like Feigelson's patient (see chapter 8), in his mother's mansion the floors leak and the walls are drafty alerts him at least to his own shortcomings in social experience. I would claim that his difficulties do not result from what his mother did to him, but, rather, that with her he failed to experience appropriately the nuances of human intercourse. Even if therapy reduces his anxiety, he will remain inadequate in intimate social contacts, unless he learns about his own scotomata in perception. Largely, the function of the transference is not to show the patient that he is projecting distortion onto the therapist but to show him that, in interaction with the therapist, he is *like* his mother. We go from asking what has been done to the patient to asking what has been the communicational nexus of which he was part. Lineal cause-effect is replaced by a systems approach. No longer focused on the "who is doing what to whom," we note that, as William Blake put it, the patient "has become what he beheld."

To review the thesis: Freud, following Breuer, came upon a novel therapy. By talking with a patient in a highly constrained setting, he was able to alleviate neurotic symptoms. The instrument of therapy was language, particularly a free-associative language; that is, rambling, free-floating, and without focused intent. Freud attributed the success of this method to *what* was talked about, not the semiotic act. What was talked about was childhood experience: first, that something terrible had happened to the child. Freud subsequently made a complete reversal and decided that nothing had been done to the child—it was his own fantasies blowing real experience out of all proportion. Why he did this has been vociferously debated by a number of revisionist psychohistorians.

As I elaborated in chapter 2, claiming that Freud had fled

from his first truth, these theorists reversed direction again, returning to a more sophisticated version of the original premise. Terrible things were done to the child by the parent, but they were covert, subtle. Freud, it was claimed, traumatized by his father's "fault" and forbidden to see what he saw, retreated from his first insight—namely, that parents damage their children. But to sustain this revisionist position, one must attribute to the parents a degree of intentionality and destructiveness that is, I suspect, as much a mythology as the original theory of infantile seduction. I also suspect that many patients do not, in their hearts, really believe it. They consider the assault on the parents part of the game of psychoanalysis, somehow necessary to the cure but not to be taken altogether literally. I have seen several patients who complained about horrendous (and documentable) deprivations by a parent but have years later met patient and parent together and observed, to my astonishment, a warm and apparently intimate relationship. Children have a very considerable capacity for compassion and forgiveness.

Sullivan, spearheading what was essentially a social psychology perspective, introduced an entirely new paradigm, an informational or communicational one. According to Kuhn, these two models would have ordinarily coexisted without much interaction until finally the older paradigm faded out, along with its epigones, or until sufficient incompatible data (data collected from the *new* perspective) made the old untenable. This did not happen, however. Sullivan attempted to bridge the two models, melding his informational model to the Freudian one. As I have indicated, his most coherent theorizing took place before 1930 in a milieu of American institutional psychiatry, as he tapped empirical and pragmatic philosophical sources and the burgeoning social sciences, particularly ethnology, linguistics, and sociology. Encouraged to pick up the psychoanalytic scepter, Sullivan attempted a fusion of two paradigms and cre-

ated a chimera: half old-world and half new. As I suggested in the clinical material, this putting a new model to the services of the old has been continued by otherwise astute clinical observers.

Is it possible to have a psychoanalysis without drives, defenses, and warped perception? If one defines the essence of psychoanalysis as being the psychoanalytic praxis, dictated by the algorithm I've outlined, then it becomes possible to discard the mechanical paradigm and aim for a purely communicational model. *One then rejects a world in which effects are brought about by forces and impacts and entertains a new world in which effects are brought about by patterns of perceived variation.* As Bateson put it:

> We must change our whole way of thinking about mental and communicational process. The ordinary analogies of energy theory which people borrow from the hard sciences to provide a conceptual framework upon which they try to build theories about psychology and behavior—that entire Procrustean structure—is non-sense. It is in error.[18]

From the communicational perspective, man is seen not only as living in a symbolic universe but as being a symbol. His capacity to comprehend and manipulate symbols defines competence and what we call his mental health. We live literally in a world of appearances, since the world is apprehended only indirectly through a series of afferent inputs. All we know of the world is what we can perceive and collate, and all we can collate are pattern, and modulations of difference. Again, as Bateson put it, following Alfred Korzybski's axiom that the map is never the territory: "Always the process of representation will filter it out so that the mental world is only maps of maps of maps, ad infinitum. All 'phenomena' are literally 'appearances.' "[19]

There is, then, an infinite regress of data. Yet, pace Bateson's clarity of presentation, when it comes to Harold's mother she is invested with "force," the capacity to destroy. I believe that a change of paradigm requires a more radical change of perception: she is not destructive or powerful but disabled, semiotically crippled. The mother of Bateson's patient is as disabled by her semiotic defect, her inability to "catch" Bateson's meaning as would be a frog unable to catch flies because his perception of motion had been damaged.

Sullivan allegedly said that psychoanalysis was like a flashlight beam projected on the patient's life; the function of the therapist was to broaden the beam, enlarging the circle of awareness. This is a purely informational simile. In the clinical material I have presented, the fallacy lies not so much in being wrong in interpretation but in *stopping short* of the next circle of awareness, of pursuing what I have referred to as the infinite regress of the psychoanalytic inquiry. The larger and wider the patient's perspective, the better equipped he is to live in the real world; not the neat, contained, nursery world of hermeneutic doctrine, but the wider, infinitely more erratic, and perplexing world in which we meet and discover ourselves in each other. This is, I think, the true crossroads—the Phocis where the paths diverge.

NOTES

Preface

1. Paul Valéry, *An Anthology*, ed. J. Lawler, J. Bollingen Series KLV. A (Princeton, N.J.: Princeton University Press, 1956), p 49.
2. Donald Spence, *Narrative Truth and Historical Truth: Meaning and Interpretation in Psychoanalysis* (New York: W.W. Norton, 1982).

Chapter 1

1. Robert J. Campbell, *Psychiatric Dictionary*, 5th ed. (New York: Oxford University Press, 1981), p. 386.
2. Anna Freud, *Difficulties in the Path of Psychoanalysis* (New York: International Universities Press, 1969), p. 49.
3. Masud Khan, "Exorcism of the Intrusive Ego-Alien Factors in the Analytic Situation and Process," in *Tactics and Techniques in Psychoanalytic Therapy*, ed. Peter Giovacchini (New York: Science House, 1972), p. 383.
4. Khan, "Exorcism," p. 384.
5. Ibid., p. 385.
6. Edgar Levenson, *The Fallacy of Understanding* (New York: Basic Books, 1972).

Chapter 2

1. Max Schur, *Freud: Living and Dying* (New York: International Universities Press, 1972); and Marie Bonaparte, Anna Freud, and Ernst Kris, *The Origins of Psychoanalysis: Letters to Wilhelm Fliess, Drafts and Notes 1887–1902*, trans. Eric Mosbacher and James Strachey (New York: Basic Books, 1954).
2. Milton Klein and David Tribich, "On Freud's Blindness," *Colloquium* 2 (2): 52–59; Marianne Krüll, *Freud und Sein Vater* (Munich: C. H. Beck, 1979); Marie Balmary, *Psychoanalyzing Psychoanalysis: Freud and the Hidden Fault of the Father* (Baltimore: Johns Hopkins Press, 1982); and R. Greenberg and C. Perlman, "If Freud Only Knew: A Reconsideration of Psychoanalytic Dream Theory," *International Review of Psychoanalysis* 5: 71–75.
3. Balmary, *Psychoanalyzing Psychoanalysis*, p. 165.
4. Erik Erikson, "Psychological Reality and Historical Actuality," in *Insight and Responsibility* (New York: W.W. Norton, 1964).
5. Sophie Freud Lowenstein, "Review of *Freud and und Sein Vater*," *Family Process* 19 (3): 307–13.

Notes

6. Balmary, *Psychoanalyzing Psychoanalysis*, p. 80.

7. Max Schur, *Freud: Living and Dying.*

8. Sigmund Freud, *The Interpretation of Dreams. The Standard Edition of the Complete Psychological Works of Sigmund Freud*, vol. 4, ed. and trans. James Strachey (London: Hogarth Press), pp. 106–21.

9. Charles Rycroft, *The Innocence of Dreams* (New York: Pantheon Books, 1979).

10. Frank Sulloway, *Freud: Biologist of the Mind* (New York: Basic Books, 1979), p. 147.

11. Morton Schatzman, *Soul Murder: Persecution in the Family* (New York: Random House, 1973).

12. Jean-Paul Sartre, *Existential Psychoanalysis* (New York: Philosophical Library, 1953).

13. Peter Giovacchini, ed., *Tactics and Techniques in Psychoanalysis* (New York: Science House, 1972), p. xiii.

14. Louise Kaplan, "The Development and Genetic Perspectives of a Life History," Presentation to the W. A. White Psychoanalytic Society, New York, October 19, 1979.

Chapter 3

1. Balmary, *Psychoanalyzing Psychoanalysis*, p. 154.

2. Gregory Bateson, *Mind and Nature: A Necessary Unity* (New York, E. P. Dutton, 1979), p. 87.

3. Schur, *Freud: Living and Dying;* Greenberg and Perlman, "If Freud Only Knew"; and Balmary, *Psychoanalyzing Psychoanalysis.*

4. Jones, *The Life and Work of Sigmund Freud: Vol. 1*, p. 19.

5. Adam Kuper and Alan Stone, "The Dream of Irma's Injection: A Structural Analysis," *American Journal of Psychiatry* 139 (10): 1225 ff.

6. Kuper and Stone, "The Dream of Irma's Injection," p. 1229.

7. Tania and James Stern, trans., *The Letters of Sigmund Freud* (New York: Basic Books, 1960), letter no. 61, p. 141.

8. Ernest Jones, *The Life and Work of Sigmund Freud: Vol. 2, 1901–1919.* (New York: Basic Books, 1955).

9. Jorge Luis Borges, *The Book of Imaginary Beings* (New York: Avon, 1969), p. 211.

10. Robert Graves, *Greek Myths* (New York: George Braziller, 1955), pp. 105.

Chapter 4

1. Anthony Wilden, *System and Structure: Essays in Communication and Exchange* (London: Tavistock Press, 1972).

2. Charles Morris, *Signs, Language and Behaviour* (Englewood Cliffs, New Jersey: Prentice-Hall).

3. Jerome Bruner, "Communication and Self," Presentation to the W.A. White Psychoanalytic Society, November 19, 1982.

4. Ibid.

Notes

Chapter 5

1. Karl Menninger and Phillip Holzman, *Theory of Psychoanalytic Technique*, 2nd ed. (New York: Basic Books, 1973), p. 8.
2. Roy Schafer, *Language and Insight* (New Haven: Yale University Press, 1978), p. 179.
3. Patrick Mullahy, *Oedipus Myth and Complex* (New York: Hermitage Press, 1948), pp. 286–91.
4. Alice Miller, *Prisoners of Childhood* (New York: Basic Books, 1981), p. 7.
5. Laurence Epstein in Arthur Feiner, "The Therapeutic Function of Hate in the Countertransference," in *Countertransference* (New York: Aronson, 1979).
6. Ludwig Eidelberg, quoted by Heinz Kohut, "Clinical and Theoretical Aspects of Resistance," *Journal of the American Psychoanalytic Association* 5 (1979):551.
7. Harry Stack Sullivan, *The Psychiatric Interview* ed. Helen S. Perry and Mary L. Gawel, (New York: W.W. Norton, 1954), pp. 21–22.
8. Leston L. Havens, *Approaches to the Mind* (Boston: Little, Brown, 1973).
9. Menninger and Holzman, *Psychoanalytic Technique*, p. 155.

Chapter 6

1. Frederick Crews, Letter to the *New York Review of Books*, Feb. 5, 1976, p. 34.
2. Gregory Bateson, "A Theory of Play and Phantasy," in *Steps Towards an Ecology of Mind* (New York: Ballantine Books, 1972).
3. Masud Khan, "To Hear with Eyes: Clinical Notes on Body as Subject and Object," in *The Privacy of the Self* (New York: International Universities Press, 1974), p. 234 ff.
4. Martin Buber, "Distance and Relation," W.A. White Memorial Lectures, 4th series, *Psychiatry* 20 (1957).
5. Bateson, *Steps*, p. 186.
6. Ibid., p. 191.

Chapter 7

1. Lionel Trilling, "Freud and Literature," in *The Liberal Imagination* (New York: Viking Press, 1951), p. 53.
2. Masud Khan, quoted in preface to Marion Milner, *The Hands of the Living God* (New York: International Universities Press, 1969), p. xxxi.

Chapter 8

1. Charles Feigelson, "Dream Experience, Analytic Experience," *The Psychoanalytic Study of the Child* 33 (1978): 366 ff.
2. Ibid., p. 363.
3. Ibid., p. 364.

Notes

4. Leo Stone, "On Resistance to the Psychoanalytic Process," in *Psychoanalysis and Contemporary Science*, ed. Helen S. Perry and Mary L. Gawel, (New York: W.W. Norton, 1973), p. 58; and Paul Ricoeur, "The Question of Proof in Freud's Writings," *Journal of the American Psychoanalytic Association* 25 (1977): 838.

5. Sigmund Freud, "Remembering, Repeating and Working Through," *Standard Edition*, vol. 12, ed. and trans. James Strachey (London: Hogarth Press, 1914), pp. 147–56.

6. Ibid.

7. Ferdinand de Saussure, "On the Nature of Language," in *Introduction to Structuralism*, ed. Michael Lane, (New York: Basic Books 1970), p. 43.

8. Walker Percy, *The Message in the Bottle* (New York: Farrar, Straus and Giroux, 1954).

9. Jacques Lacan, *Écrits* (New York: W.W. Norton, 1977).

10. Gregory Bateson, *Communication: The Social Matrix of Psychiatry* (New York: W.W. Norton, 1951), p. 23.

11. Harry Stack Sullivan, *The Interpersonal Theory of Psychiatry*, ed. Helen S. Perry and Mary L. Gawel (New York: W.W. Norton, 1953).

12. P. F. Strawson, "On Referring," in *Philosophy and Ordinary Language*, ed. Charles Caton (Chicago: University of Illinois Press).

13. Marshall Edelson, *Language and Interpretation in Psychoanalysis* (New Haven: Yale University Press, 1975), p. 63.

14. Ralph R. Greenson, *The Technique and Practice of Psychoanalysis* (New York: International Universities Press, 1976), pp. 272–73.

15. Gerald Chrzanowski, *Interpersonal Approach to Psychoanalysis: A Contemporary View of Harry Stack Sullivan* (New York: Gardner Press, 1977).

16. Otto Kernberg, *Borderline Conditions and Pathological Narcissism* (New York: Aronson, 1975); Heinz Kohut, "The Analysis of the Self: A Systematic Approach to the Psychoanalytic Treatment of Narcissistic Personality Disorders," *Monograph Series of the Psychoanalytic Study of the Child*, no. 4 (New York: International Universities Press, 1971); Hyman Muslin and Morton Gill, "Transference in the Dora Case" *Journal of the American Psychoanalytic Association* 26 (1978): 311–28; and Schafer, *Language and Insight*.

17. Roland Barthes, "To Write: An Intransitive Verb?" in *The Structuralist Controversy*, ed. Richard Macksey and Eugenio Donato (Baltimore: Johns Hopkins Press, 1970), p. 136.

Chapter 9

1. Masud Khan, Introduction to Milner, *Hands of the Living God*.

2. Jay Haley, *Strategies of Psychotherapy* (New York: Grune and Stratton, 1967).

3. Paul Dewald, *The Psychoanalytic Process: A Case Illustration* (New York: Basic Books, 1972).

4. Samuel Lipton, "A Critical Review," *Contemporary Psychoanalysis* 18 (1982): 349–66.

Chapter 10

1. Erich Fromm, *The Forgotten Language* (New York: Rinehart and Co., 1951).

2. Jones, *Life and Work of Freud: Vol 1.*, p. 180.

3. Milton Erickson, *Ericksonian Approaches to Hypnosis and Psychotherapy,* ed. Jeffrey Zeig (New York: Brunner/Mazel, 1982).

4. Lionel Trilling, *Sincerity and Authenticity* (Cambridge, Mass: Harvard University Press, 1972).

5. Donald Meltzer, "Routine and Inspired Interpretations," *Contemporary Psychoanalysis* 14 (1978): 210–24. Reprinted in Epstein and Feiner, *Countertransference.*

Chapter 11

1. Alvin Frank, "Two Theories or One? Or None?" *Journal of the American Psychoanalytic Association* 27 (1979): 169–207.

2. Schafer, *Language and Insight,* p. 184.

3. Muslin and Gill, *Dora Case,* p. 327.

4. Aldo Carotenuto, *A Secret Symmetry,* trans. Arno Pomerans, John Sheply, and Krishna Winston (New York: Pantheon Books, 1982).

5. Felix Deutsch, "A Footnote to Freud's 'Fragment of an Analysis of a Case of Hysteria,' " *Psychoanalytic Quarterly* 26 (1957): 159–67.

6. Charles Hampden-Turner, *Maps of the Mind* (New York: Collier, 1981), pp. 80–83.

7. Sulloway, *Freud: Biologist of the Mind,* pp. 147–50.

8. Silvano Arieti, *The Intrapsychic Self* (New York: Basic Books, 1967).

9. Hampden-Turner, *Maps.*

10. Ludwig Von Bertalanffy, *Organismic Psychology and Systems Theory,* vol 1., 1966 Heinz Werner Lecture Series. (Barre, Mass: Clark University Press, 1968).

11. Hampden-Turner, *Maps.*

12. Sullivan, *The Interpersonal Theory of Psychiatry,* pp. 341–42.

13. Helen S. Perry, *Psychiatrist of America: The Life of Harry Stack Sullivan* (Cambridge, Mass: Harvard University Press, 1982), pp. 336–37.

14. Bateson, *Mind and Nature.*

15. Alfred Korzybski, *Time-Binding: The General Theory* (Lakeville, Conn.: Institute of General Semantics, 1954).

Chapter 12

1. Kenneth L. Chatelaine, *Harry Stack Sullivan: The Formative Years* (Washington, D.C.: University Press of America, 1981), p. iv.

2. Sulloway, *Freud: Biologist of the Mind.*

3. Thomas Kuhn, *The Structure of Scientific Revolutions* (Chicago: University of Chicago Press, 1962).

4. R. D. Laing, *The Politics of Experience* (New York: Pantheon Books, 1967).

5. Perry, *Life of Harry Stack Sullivan,* p. 225.

6. Ibid., p. 226.

7. Ibid., p. 182.

8. Chatelaine, *Formative Years,* p. 463.

9. Ibid., p. 411.

10. Chrzanowski, *Interpersonal Approach.*

11. Sullivan, *Interpersonal Theory,* p. 8.

12. Campbell, *Psychiatric Dictionary.*

Notes

13. Rollo May, *The Meaning of Anxiety* (New York: Washington Square Press, 1979), p. 50.

14. Sullivan, *Interpersonal Theory*, p. 103.

15. Sullivan, *Conceptions of Modern Psychiatry* (New York: W.W. Norton, 1953), p. 133.

16. Sigmund Freud, *Beyond the Pleasure Principle*, ed. and trans. James Strachey. *Standard Edition* (New York: W.W. Norton, 1961), pp. 8–11.

17. Lacan, *Écrits*, p. 163.

18. Chrzanowski, *Interpersonal Approach*.

19. Harry Stack Sullivan, *The Psychiatric Interview* (New York: W.W. Norton, 1954), p. 217.

20. Sullivan, *Interpersonal Theory*, p. 165.

21. John Lincourt and Paul Olczack, "C.S. Peirce and H.S. Sullivan on the Human Self," *Psychiatry* 37 (1974): 78–87.

22. Sullivan, *Interpersonal Theory*, p. 343.

23. Perry, *Life of Harry Stack Sullivan*, p. 189.

24. Sullivan, *Interpersonal Theory*, pp. 337–38.

25. Ibid., p. 334.

26. Perry, *Life of Harry Stack Sullivan*, p. 190.

27. Sullivan, *Interpersonal Theory*, p. 335.

28. Perry, *Life of Harry Stack Sullivan*, p. 37.

29. Chatelaine, *Formative Years*, p. 305.

30. Ibid., p. 406.

31. Epstein and Feiner, *Countertransference*.

32. David Greene, trans., *Oedipus Rex*, in *Complete Greek Tragedies: Vol. 2, Sophocles*, ed. David Greene and Richard Lattimore (Chicago: University of Chicago Press, 1941), p. 29.

Chapter 13

1. Steven Mitchell, "The Origin and Nature of the Object in the Theories of Klein and Fairbairn," *Contemporary Psychoanalysis* 17 (1981): 378.

2. Milton Klein and David Tribich, "Kernberg's Object-Relations Theory: A Critical Evaluation, *International Journal of Psychoanalysis* 62 (1981): 27 ff.

3. Mitchell, "Origin and Nature."

4. Jay S. Kwawer, "Object-Relations Theory and Intimacy," in *Intimacy*, ed. Martin Fisher and George Stricker (New York: Plenum, 1982).

5. James Grotstein, "Newer Perspectives in Object Relationship Therapy," *Contemporary Psychoanalysis* 18 (1982): 71–72.

6. Donald Meltzer, "The Relations of Splitting of Attention to Splitting of Self and Objects," *Contemporary* Psychoanalysis 17 (1981): 232–38.

Chapter 14

1. Schatzman, *Soul Murder*.

2. Sullivan, *Interpersonal Theory*, p. 373.

3. Ibid., p. 341.

4. Bateson, *Steps,* p. 198.

5. Ibid., p. 217.

6. Ibid., p. 199.

7. Schatzman, *Soul Murder,* p. 154.

8. Sullivan, *The Fusion of Psychiatry and Social Science* (New York: W.W. Norton, 1964).

9. Clara Thompson, *Interpersonal Psychoanalysis: Selected Papers of Clara Thompson,* ed. Maurice Green (New York: Basic Books, 1964).

10. Irena Klenbort, "Another Look at Sullivan's Concept of Individuality," *Contemporary Psychoanalysis* 14 (1978):1.

11. Noam Chomsky, *Language and Mind* (New York: Harcourt Brace Jovanovich, 1972).

12. Fyodor Dostoyevsky, *Notes from Underground,* ed. Andrew McAndrew (New York: Signet, 1961).

13. May, *Meaning of Anxiety.*

14. Ibid., p. 223.

15. Ibid., p. 224.

16. Ibid., p. 224–25.

17. Ibid., p. 52.

18. Bateson, *Steps,* p. 453.

19. Ibid., pp. 455–56.

INDEX

acting-out, 84; *see also* countertransference
Alexander, 29
algorithm(s): linguistic, 9; psychoanalytic, 9, 11; resonance of, vs. content, 9
American institutional psychiatry, 127
American pragmatic psychoanalytic movement, 11; *see also* Sullivan, Harry Stack
anal retentiveness: Freud on, 63
anger: in parent-child relationship, 44, 68; in patient-therapist interaction, 69
anxiety: Bateson on, 152; in childhood, 37, 39, 128–31; and emotional disturbance, 157; and fantasy, 36; Freud on, 36, 132, 152; Kierkegaard on, 158; and language, 132, 133; Levenson on, 133; in patient-therapist interaction, 49; and sexual feelings, 39; Sullivan on, 36, 39, 128–30, 131–32, 133, 141, 142, 152, 154; in therapy, 49
aphasics: rage in, 132–33
Apollo, 28
Arieti, Silvano, *Intrapsychic Self, The*, 113
Aristotle, 54
Athena, 138

Balmary, Marie, *Psychoanalyzing Psychoanalysis: Freud and the Hidden Fault of the Father*, 16, 18, 23, 25
bank loan, as dream symbol, 64
Barthes, Roland, "To Write: An Intransitive Verb?," 88
Bateson, Gregory: on anxiety, 152; *Communication: The Social Matrix of Psychiatry*, 81; double-bind theory of schizophrenia of, 150–51, 152, 164; *Mind and Nature: A Necessary Unity*,

23, 121; *Steps Towards an Ecology of Mind*, 150–51, 152, 163, 164; "Theory of Play and Phantasy, A," 56, 59, 60
behavior: as conflict, 22, 30; language as, 83; as language, 88
beheading, as dream symbol, 144
Bion, Wilfred, 6, 140
birth trauma dream, 144
blacksmith, as dream symbol, 45
Blake, William, 161
boat, capsizing, as dream symbol, 3–4
Bonaparte, Marie; Freud, Anna; and Kris, Ernst, *Origins of Psychoanalysis: Letters to Wilhelm Fliess, The*, 15
Bowlby, John, 140
breast feeding, 129, 142–43, 158–60
Brenner, Charles, 59
Breuer, Josef, 8, 161
British Psychoanalytic Society, 107
Broca's area, 114
Brown, Harold, case (May), 158–61, 164
Bruner, Jerome, "Communication and Self," 35, 37
Buber, Martin, 90; "Distance and Relation," 58–59
bull, as dream symbol, 73–75

Carotenuto, Aldo, *Secret Symmetry, A*, 110–11
Carroll, Lewis: *Alice in Wonderland*, 32; *Through the Looking-Glass*, 32
castration, 29, 157; symbolic, 105, 150
castration anxiety, 33, 41, 75
causality, 40
Chapman, Ross McClure, 127, 136, 137
Chatelaine, Kenneth L., *Harry Stack Sullivan: The Formative Years*, 124, 128, 137
child(ren), 39, 43, 70; anxiety in, 37, 39,

Index

Index

Index

Index

Sullivan, Harry Stack *(continued)*
der as symbol for, 126–27, 126n, 133–34, 136, 137; spider dream of, 126, 133–34, 136–37; syntaxic mode, 40, 127, 142; on terror, 136; therapeutic concept of, 51–52, 99, 156, 164; and Tiresias, 138; and Twain's *Mysterious Stranger*, 119–20; unfinished work of, 124; writings about, 124, 125–26, 128, 132, 133, 137, 154

Sullivanians, 10; and therapeutic process, 62

Sulloway, Frank, *Freud: Biologist of the Mind*, 19, 112–13, 124n

superego, 46

symbolism: Freud on, 30–31

symbolization, 14, 20, 21, 132

syntaxic mode, 40, 127, 142

teaching, as armature for learning, 5

terror: language as defense against, 132, 136; Sullivan on, 132, 136

therapeutic concept: of Sullivan, 51–52, 99, 156, 164; *see also* psychoanalysis: interpersonal

therapist(s): directive, 104; as dream symbol, 106–8, 144; family, 15, 45, 50, 101, 105; as father, 69; interpersonal, 16, 21, 51, 103, 105, 106, 147; trustworthiness of, 48; as validator, 52; *see also* psychoanalyst

Thompson, Clara, 127; *Selected Papers*, 154

Tiresias, 138

transference, 4, 21, 51, 59, 63, 68, 76, 78, 83, 84, 91, 107, 115, 116, 143, 144, 145, 157; distortion of, 96; and dreams, 78; erotic, 60; Freud on, 8, 59, 68, 95; function of, 161; importance of, 55; negative, 102; positive, 60, 106;

validity of, 46; *see also* countertransference

trauma(s), 23, 24; birth, 144

Trilling, Lionel: "Freud and Literature," 63; *Sincerity and Authenticity*, 104n

Twain, Mark, *Mysterious Stranger, The*, 119–20

unconscious, 115; collusion of, in sexuality, 65; fantasy in, 66; and psychological reality, 13

Valéry, Paul, *ix*

Von Bertalaffny, Ludwig, *Organismic Psychology and Systems Theory*, 113–14

Vulcan, 45

Washoe (chimpanzee), 80n

Weltanschauung, of psychoanalysts, 6

White, William Alanson, 127, 135, 137

White Institute, 102

Whitehead, Alfred North, 159

Whittier, John Greenleaf, 132

Wilde, Oscar, 44

Wilden, Anthony, *System and Structure*, 80

Winnicott, Donald, 43, 140, 141, 143

wish fulfillment, 43

Wittgenstein, Ludwig, 71, 88

World War I, 100

Zeus, 138

Zipa, 45